Heritage Signature® Auction #6042
Natural History

June 6, 2010 | Beverly Hills, California

Y0-CXM-103

LOT VIEWING

Heritage Auction Galleries
9478 W. Olympic Blvd., First Floor • Beverly Hills, CA 90212

Thursday, June 3 - Saturday, June 5, 2010
10:00 AM – 6:00 PM PT

Sunday, June 6, 2010 • 10:00 AM – 1:00 PM PT

View Lots Online at HA.com/6042

LIVE FLOOR BIDDING
Bid in person during the floor sessions.

LIVE TELEPHONE BIDDING *(floor sessions only)*
Phone bidding must be arranged on or before
Friday, June 4, 2010, by 12:00 PM CT.
Client Service: 866-835-3243.

HERITAGE Live!™ BIDDING
Bid live from your location, anywhere in the world,
during the Auction using our HERITAGE Live!™ program
at HA.com/Live

INTERNET BIDDING
Internet absentee bidding ends at 10:00 PM CT
the evening before the session. HA.com/6042

FAX BIDDING
Fax bids must be received on or before Friday,
June 4, 2010, by 12:00 PM CT. Fax: 214-409-1425

MAIL BIDDING
Mail bids must be received on or before
Friday, June 4, 2010.

*Please see "Choose Your Bidding Method" in the back of this
catalog for specific details about each of these bidding methods.*

LIVE AUCTION
SIGNATURE® FLOOR SESSION 1
(Floor, Telephone, HERITAGE Live!,™ Internet, Fax, and Mail)

Heritage Auction Galleries
9478 W. Olympic Blvd., First Floor • Beverly Hills, CA 90212

SESSION 1
Sunday, June 6, 2010 • 1:00 PM PT • Lots 49001–49257

AUCTION RESULTS
Immediately available at HA.com/6042

LOT SETTLEMENT AND PICK-UP
Available immediately following session or
Monday, June 7 - Wednesday, June 9 • 9:00 AM- 5:00 PM PT
by appointment only at the Beverly Hills Office.

All other pick-ups starting Monday June 14
9:00 AM – 5:00 PM CT by appointment only
at the Dallas office.

Extended Payment Terms available. See details in the back of this catalog.

*Lots are sold at an approximate rate of 60 lots per hour, but it
is not uncommon to sell 45 lots or 90 lots in any given hour.*

This auction is subject to a 19.5% Buyer's Premium.

Heritage Numismatic Auctions, Inc.: CA Bond #RSB2004175; CA Auctioneer Bonds:
Samuel Foose #RSB2004178; Robert Korver #RSB2004179; Bob Merrill #RSB2004177;
Leo Frese #RSB2004176; Jeff Engelken #RSB2004180; Jacob Walker #RSB2005394;
Scott Peterson #RSB2005395; Shaunda Fry #RSB2005396; Mike Sadler #RSB2005412;
Andrea Voss #RSB2004676; Teia Baber #RSB2005525.

THIS AUCTION IS PRESENTED AND CATALOGED BY HERITAGE AUCTIONS, INC.

Heritage World Headquarters

HERITAGE HA.com
Auction Galleries

Home Office • 3500 Maple Avenue, 17th Floor • Dallas, TX 75219
Design District Annex • 1518 Slocum Street • Dallas, TX 75207
Beverly Hills Office • 9478 W. Olympic Blvd., First Floor • Beverly Hills, CA 90212
214.528.3500 | 800.872.6467 | 214.409.1425 (fax)
Direct Client Service Line: Toll Free 1.866.835.3243 • Email: Bid@HA.com

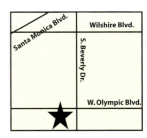

Beverly Hills Office
9478 W. Olympic Blvd., First Floor
Beverly Hills, CA. 90212

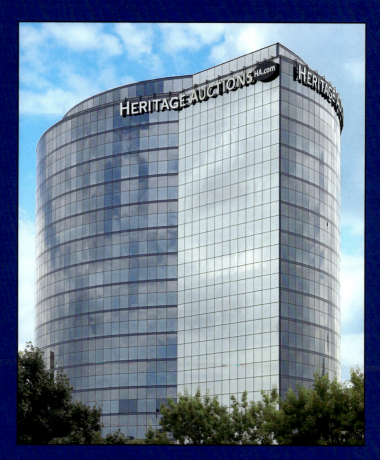

DIRECTORY FOR DEPARTMENT SPECIALISTS AND SERVICES

COINS & CURRENCY

COINS – UNITED STATES
HA.com/Coins

Leo Frese, Ext. 1294
Leo@HA.com
David Mayfield, Ext. 1277
DavidM@HA.com
Jessica Aylmer, Ext. 1706
JessicaA@HA.com
Diedre Buchmoyer, Ext. 1794
DiedreB@HA.com
Win Callender, Ext. 1415
WinC@HA.com
Katherine Crippe, Ext. 1389
KK@HA.com
Chris Dykstra, Ext. 1380
ChrisD@HA.com
Sam Foose, Ext. 1227
SamF@HA.com
Jason Friedman, Ext. 1582
JasonF@HA.com
Shaunda Fry, Ext. 1159
ShaundaF@HA.com
Jim Jelinski, Ext. 1257
JimJ@HA.com
Bob Marino, Ext. 1374
BobMarino@HA.com
Mike Sadler, Ext. 1332
MikeS@HA.com
Beau Streicher, Ext. 1645
BeauS@HA.com

RARE CURRENCY
HA.com/Currency

Len Glazer, Ext. 1390
Len@HA.com
Allen Mincho, Ext. 1327
Allen@HA.com
Dustin Johnston, Ext. 1302
Dustin@HA.com
Michael Moczalla, Ext. 1481
MichaelM@HA.com
Jason Friedman, Ext. 1582
JasonF@HA.com

WORLD & ANCIENT COINS
HA.com/WorldCoins

Warren Tucker, Ext. 1287
WTucker@HA.com
Cristiano Bierrenbach, Ext. 1661
CrisB@HA.com
Scott Cordry, Ext. 1369
ScottC@HA.com

COMICS & COMIC ART
HA.com/Comics

Ed Jaster, Ext. 1288
EdJ@HA.com
Lon Allen, Ext. 1261
LonA@HA.com
Barry Sandoval, Ext. 1377
BarryS@HA.com
Todd Hignite, Ext. 1790
ToddH@HA.com

FINE ART

AMERICAN & EUROPEAN PAINTINGS & SCULPTURE
HA.com/FineArt

Ed Jaster, Ext. 1288
EdJ@HA.com
Courtney Case, Ext. 1293
CourtneyC@HA.com
Marianne Berardi, Ph.D., Ext. 1506
MarianneB@HA.com
Ariana Hartsock, Ext. 1283
ArianaH@HA.com

ART OF THE AMERICAN WEST
HA.com/WesternArt
Michael Duty, Ext. 1712
MichaelD@HA.com

FURNITURE & DECORATIVE ART
HA.com/Decorative
Tim Rigdon, Ext. 1119
TimR@HA.com
Karen Rigdon, Ext. 1723
KarenR@HA.com
Nicholas Dawes, Ext. 1605
NickD@HA.com

ILLUSTRATION ART
HA.com/Illustration
Ed Jaster, Ext. 1288
EdJ@HA.com
Todd Hignite, Ext. 1790
ToddH@HA.com

MODERN & CONTEMPORARY ART
HA.com/Modern
Frank Hettig, Ext. 1157
FrankH@HA.com

SILVER & VERTU
HA.com/Silver
Tim Rigdon, Ext. 1119
TimR@HA.com
Karen Rigdon, Ext. 1723
KarenR@HA.com

TEXAS ART
HA.com/TexasArt
Atlee Phillips, Ext. 1786
AtleeP@HA.com

20TH-CENTURY DESIGN
HA.com/Design
Tim Rigdon, Ext. 1119
TimR@HA.com
Karen Rigdon, Ext. 1723
KarenR@HA.com
Nicholas Dawes, Ext. 1605
NickD@HA.com

VINTAGE & CONTEMPORARY PHOTOGRAPHY
HA.com/ArtPhotography
Ed Jaster, Ext. 1288
EdJ@HA.com
Kelly Jones, Ext. 1166
KellyJ@HA.com

HISTORICAL

AMERICAN INDIAN ART
HA.com/AmericanIndian
Delia Sullivan, Ext. 1343
DeliaS@HA.com

AMERICANA & POLITICAL
HA.com/Historical
Tom Slater, Ext. 1441
TomS@HA.com
John Hickey, Ext. 1264
JohnH@HA.com
Michael Riley, Ext. 1467
MichaelR@HA.com

CIVIL WAR AND ARMS & MILITARIA
HA.com/CivilWar
Dennis Lowe, Ext. 1182
DennisL@HA.com

HISTORICAL MANUSCRIPTS
HA.com/Manuscripts
Sandra Palomino, Ext. 1107
SandraP@HA.com

RARE BOOKS
HA.com/Books
James Gannon, Ext. 1609
JamesG@HA.com
Joe Fay, Ext. 1544
JoeF@HA.com

SPACE EXPLORATION
HA.com/Space
John Hickey, Ext. 1264
JohnH@HA.com
Michael Riley, Ext. 1467
MichaelR@HA.com

TEXANA
HA.com/Historical
Sandra Palomino, Ext. 1107
SandraP@HA.com

JEWELRY & TIMEPIECES

FINE JEWELRY
HA.com/Jewelry
Jill Burgum, Ext. 1697
JillB@HA.com

WATCHES & FINE TIMEPIECES
HA.com/Timepieces
Jim Wolf, Ext. 1659
JWolf@HA.com

MUSIC & ENTERTAINMENT MEMORABILIA
HA.com/Entertainment
Doug Norwine, Ext. 1452
DougN@HA.com
John Hickey, Ext. 1264
JohnH@HA.com
Garry Shrum, Ext. 1585
GarryS@HA.com

NATURAL HISTORY
HA.com/NaturalHistory
David Herskowitz, Ext. 1610
DavidH@HA.com

RARE STAMPS
HA.com/Stamps
Steven Crippe, Ext. 1777
StevenC@HA.com

SPORTS COLLECTIBLES
HA.com/Sports

Chris Ivy, Ext. 1319
CIvy@HA.com
Peter Calderon, Ext. 1789
PeterC@HA.com
Mike Gutierrez, Ext. 1183
MikeG@HA.com
Lee Iskowltz, Ext. 1601
LeeI@HA.com
Mark Jordan, Ext. 1187
MarkJ@HA.com
Chris Nerat, Ext. 1615
ChrisN@HA.com
Jonathan Scheier, Ext. 1314
JonathanS@HA.com

VINTAGE MOVIE POSTERS
HA.com/MoviePosters

Grey Smith, Ext. 1367
GreySm@HA.com
Bruce Carteron, Ext. 1551
BruceC@HA.com

TRUSTS & ESTATES & APPRAISAL SERVICES
HA.com/Estates
Mark Prendergast, Ext. 1632
MPrendergast@HA.com
HA.com/Appraisals
Meredith Meuwly, Ext. 1631
MeredithM@HA.com

CORPORATE & INSTITUTIONAL COLLECTIONS/VENTURES
Jared Green, Ext. 1279
Jared@HA.com

CREDIT DEPARTMENT
Marti Korver, Ext. 1248
Marti@HA.com
Eric Thomas, Ext. 1241
EricT@HA.com

MEDIA & PUBLIC RELATIONS
Noah Fleisher, Ext. 1143
NoahF@HA.com

BEVERLY HILLS OFFICE
9478 W. Olympic Blvd., First Floor
Beverly Hills, CA 90212

Leo Frese, Ext. 1294
Leo@HA.com
Michael Moline, Ext. 1361
MMoline@HA.com
Shaunda Fry, Ext. 1159
ShaundaF@HA.com
Carolyn Mani, Ext. 1605
CarolynM@HA.com

HOUSTON OFFICE
Mark Prendergast, Ext. 1632
MPrendergast@HA.com

NEW YORK OFFICE
Tiffany Dubin, Ext. 1673
TiffanyD@HA.com
Nick Dawes, Ext. 1605
NickD@HA.com

CORPORATE OFFICERS
R. Steven Ivy, Co-Chairman
James L. Halperin, Co-Chairman
Gregory J. Rohan, President
Paul Minshull, Chief Operating Officer
Todd Imhof, Executive Vice President
Leo Frese, Managing Director, Beverly Hills

TABLE OF CONTENTS

ERA	PERIOD	EPOCH	MILLION YEARS AGO
CENOZOIC	QUATERNARY	Holocene (Recent)	Present to 0.01
		Pleistocene (Ice Age)	0.01 to 2
	TERTIARY	Pliocene	2 to 5
		Miocene	5 to 25
		Oligocene	25 to 38
		Eocene	38 to 55
		Paleocene	55 to 65
MESOZOIC (Age of the Dinosaurs)	CRETACEOUS		65 to 144
	JURASSIC		144 to 213
	TRIASSIC		213 to 248
PALEOZOIC	PERMIAN		248 to 286
	CARBONIFEROUS		286 to 360
	DEVONIAN		360 to 480
	SILURIAN		408 to 438
	ORDOVICIAN		438 to 505
	CAMBRIAN		505 to 590

FLOOR, TELEPHONE, HERITAGE LIVE!™, INTERNET, FAX, AND MAIL
SIGNATURE® AUCTION #6042 • BEVERLY HILLS, CALIFORNIA
SUNDAY, JUNE 6, 2010, 1:00 PM PT • LOTS 49001-49257

A 19.5% Buyer's Premium Will Be Added To All Lots. Visit HA.com/6042 to view scalable images and bid online.

ZOOLOGY

49001   LARGE BOBCAT FULL-BODY MOUNT
Lynx rufus
Similar to the Canadian Lynx but smaller in body size and with shorter tassels on the ear tips, the American Bobcat is one of the most successful North American predators. This one came from Deep South Texas and sports a very beautiful spot pattern. The taxidermy exhibits superior quality workmanship and it is prepared in a very lifelike pose on a naturalistic base, 18¼ inches high and 38 inches long overall.
Estimate: $800-$1,200

49002   COYOTE FULL-BODY MOUNT
Canis latrans
The American Coyote is probably the smartest and most successful predator on the planet: they have been shot, trapped, poisoned, and very heavily hunted for about two hundred years and yet they still remain in very stable populations across most of North America. In some rural areas the populations are actually growing and they are even managing to exist within many city limits close to large townships. This mount is of a large male mounted in a natural habitat scene with taxidermy quality second to none, and measures 37¼ inches high and 37 inches long overall.
Estimate: $600-$1,000

49003   GREATER KUDU SHOULDER MOUNT
Tragelaphus strepsiceros strepsiceros

The Greater Kudu is an elegant and large elk-sized Antelope with magnificent corkscrew-shaped horns. These horns sometimes bear ivory tips, as is the case here (removable for easy shipping and storage). These animals are largely nocturnal, wary and alert, with hearing second to none and keen senses of sight and smell. They are often called the "Big Gray Ghost of Africa" and many a hunter has tried to sneak up on this giant-eared Antelope only to see it disappear into the African Bushveld. This mount has a handsome lifelike pose and excellent taxidermy quality, measuring 34½ inches from the wall to the tip of the nose, 60 inches high overall and 22⅝ inches between the horn tips.

Estimate: $900-$1,500

49004   STONE SHEEP SHOULDER MOUNT
Ovis dalli stonei

The Stone Sheep is found only in British Columbia, Canada. It has been aptly described as being "A Dall Sheep in evening dress" and is easily the most beautiful of all the North American Sheep. This particular Ram is a full-curl trophy with horns that measure 38½ x 37⅝ inches long around the curl and bases each 14⅝ inches in circumference. The taxidermy quality is outstanding and the Ram has a very lifelike and alert looking pose, standing 22¼ inches from the wall, measuring 31 inches high overall and 21¾ inches between the horn tips.

Estimate: $1,850-$2,850

49005 SOUTHERN IMPALA SHOULDER MOUNT

Aepyceros melampus melampus

The Impala is the world's greatest jumper, elegant and graceful, and able to leap over 30 feet in a single bound. The Southern Impala is smaller and less bright in color than the East African species, but these animals are a sportsman's favorite and quite plentiful. The present example is a trophy Ram that will easily qualify for the Safari Club International record books; its horns measure 23½ inches long on each side and the mount is in mint condition, standing 20¾ inches from the wall to the tip of the nose, 39 inches from the bottom of the brisket to the tip of the horns and 11⅞ inches between the horn tips. A first-class trophy.

Estimate: $900-$1,500

49006 RECORD-CLASS AFRICAN WARTHOG SHOULDER MOUNT

Phacohoerus aethiopicus

The Warthog will never win an Animal Kingdom beauty contest, but they do make for wonderful Big Game. A gregarious animal, they live in bands of 4 to 6, and both males and females have warts and tusks which they use for rooting and for defense. The males grow larger than the females, and this is a trophy-class boar with real ivory tusks measuring 13¾ x 13¾ inches long, of which about 2¾ inches is inside the mouth. The taxidermy quality is outstanding and he measures 16½ inches high and 12⅛ inches between the tips of the tusks.

Estimate: $675-$975

49007 AFRICAN SACRED IBIS

Threskiornis aethiopicus

The Sacred Ibis was venerated in Ancient Egypt as a symbol of Thoth, the god that bore its head. Native now only to sub-Saharan Africa they are shoreline birds that use their long snipe-like bill to forage for food. When mature, it can reach nearly three feet in length and this is an adult male in breeding plumage, recently mounted and complete with necessary paperwork. The taxidermy quality is excellent and presented on a naturalistic base with reeds it measures 20 inches high overall.

Estimate: $550-$850

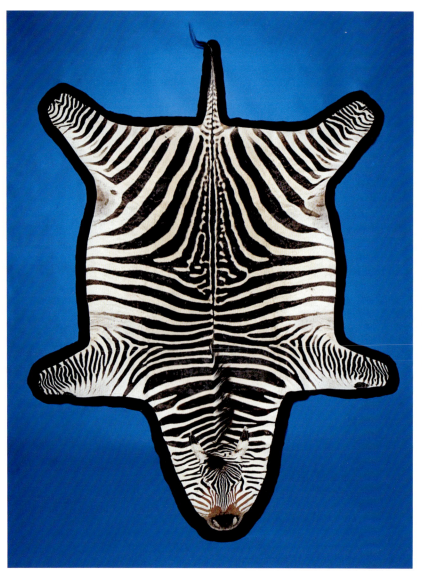

49008   EXTRA LARGE AAA ZEBRA RUG
Equus quagga burchelli
This rug is made from the skin of a fine large Stallion from southern Africa with excellent markings, few scars, and a brilliant stripe pattern. The taxidermy quality is outstanding and the padding is neatly sewn and not glued like cheaper quality rugs. It measures 9 feet, 8 inches long from nose to tip of tail and is approximately 60 inches wide across the middle of the belly.
Estimate: $1,700-$2,500

49009   PAIR OF SPERM WHALE TEETH
Physeter macrocephalus
South Pacific
Sperm Whales were hunted for a variety of commercial and industrial reasons between the 1700's and late 1900's and were extremely dangerous prey; in 1820 a large Sperm Whale sunk the whaler *Essex* and the creature entered the popular imagination for all time as inspiration for Herman Melville's *Moby Dick*. The teeth of the Sperm Whale were culturally significant objects throughout the Pacific, being used as gifts of atonement and objects of value in Fiji and Tonga. Later on, a surplus of teeth from whaling led to the art of scrimshaw – sailor's carved images in the ivory. This pair of teeth likely originated in the southeastern Pacific from the voyages of the whaling ship *Balaena*, out of New Bedford, Massachusetts. Captain John S. Dorman was Master of this ship and these teeth were from whales harvested during his second voyage, between October 5th, 1858 and July 26th, 1863. The larger of the two has a light polished to the enamel, with a naturally worn tip and hollow root, and measures 5⅛ inches around the curve. The other tooth has an excellent pointed tip, a sawn-off base with evidence of an aborted saw cut, and a light polish to its ribbed surface, 4½ inches around the outside curve, accompanied by framed display recounting their probable history.
Complete with documentation allowing it to be sold within the United States; it is important to note however that it cannot be exported outside of the United States.
Estimate: $500-$700

49010 LARGE SPERM WHALE TOOTH

Physeter macrocephalus
South Pacific

The Sperm Whale is a fascinating creature, holding the record for both being the largest toothed animal and for having the largest brain of any animal. Reaching lengths of over 65 feet and able to dive up to 9800 feet to the depths of the ocean, the Sperm Whale feeds on many forms of prey, including the Giant Squid, using its massive jaws lined with large sharp teeth. Hunting of Sperm Whales began in the early 1700's and ended (officially) in the 1980's. Valued for their spermaceti (waxy buoyancy liquid found in the head) and blubber oil for commercial and industrial uses, and precious ambergris for use as a fixative in perfumery; their teeth were usually kept as souvenirs or used for the decorative marine carvings known as scrimshaw. This impressive specimen was from the collection of Captain John S. Dorman (1819-1902), Master of the 301-ton whaling ship *Balaena* out of New Bedford, Massachusetts. The tooth is believed to have been collected during Captain Dorman's second voyage, between October 5th, 1858 and July 26th, 1863, whilst whaling between the Galapagos Islands and the coast of Chile. It is in pristine condition with a naturally worn tip and good hollow root cavity, and measures 7½ inches along the outside curve. The specimen comes with provenance documentation and a framed display describing the life of Captain Dorman and the origin of the tooth.

Complete with documentation allowing it to be sold within the United States; it is important to note however that it cannot be exported outside of the United States.
Estimate: $600-$850

49011 GIANT HUMBOLT SQUID BEAK

Dosidicus gigas
Eastern Pacific Ocean

The Humboldt, or Jumbo, Squid, is a large predatory marine cephalopod that thrives throughout the Eastern Pacific ocean. Reaching sizes of almost 6 feet in length and up to 100 lb in weight, the Humboldt squid is a large ferocious predator, its tentacles lined with hooked suckers for capturing its prey, and equipped with a sharp and deadly parrot-like beak for the rending of flesh. Adding to their deadliness is the fact that the squids have been observed hunting in packs, seeming to communicate to each other by changing their complex colors using chromatophores, cooperating to take down large prey. These intelligent squids have been known to attack divers and fishermen and even cannibalistically attack and consume their own wounded and vulnerable. This beak specimen measuring 2½ x 2 x 2½ inches and came from a large individual, very sharp and excellently preserved with the exception of a small crack.
Estimate: $600-$800

49012 NARWHAL TUSK

Monodon monoceras
Arctic Ocean

One of the strangest-looking creatures to be found on the Earth, the Narwhal is a toothed whale native to the Arctic waters of Canada and Greenland. It is immediately recognizable by the remarkable helical "horn" that protrudes from its mouth up to a length of 10 feet. This horn has inspired many myths and suppositions: the Inuit have it that the Narwhal was created when a woman with a harpoon was dragged into the ocean by the Beluga whale she had speared (the Beluga being the Narwhal's only relative in the Monodontidae family). Elsewhere it is thought to have originated the unicorn myth and in medieval Europe such horns changed hands for huge sums of money, worth more than their weight in gold and prized for supposed magical properties. Indeed, there is still some question as to their actual scientific function: usually the horn is found only in the male, a radically enlarged right incisor, although horned females are occasionally recorded (as are, rarely, double-horned specimens) so it is commonly supposed to be a secondary sexual characteristic used in courting and rutting. Recent research suggests, however, that unlike the protruding horn-like teeth and tusks found in other mammals, that of the Narwhal may in fact be a sensory organ; electron micrography reveals millions of tiny tubules leading from the surface of the horn and apparently connecting to the nervous system. Such tubules are found in many species, but do not typically extend to the outer surface of healthy teeth. As the Narwhal is a benthic feeder and one of the deepest-diving of all whales, some suppose that the horn is used to sense water temperature and pressure. Whatever it's secret, the Narwhal's horn is one of the wonders of the natural world and this is a good medium sized specimen at 63⅝ inches long which exhibits the classic left-handed helix structure all the way along its length. A small natural chip near the tip is present, otherwise in fine condition. Comes complete with a stepped circular black marble base.

Accompanied with documentation allowing it to be sold within the United States. However, it is important to note that this lot cannot be exported outside of the United States.
Estimate: $9,000-$12,000

49013 PAIR OF GIANT SAWFISH ROSTRA
Pristis sp.
Indonesia

The mysterious sawfish is immediately identifiable due to its remarkable saw-like rostrum (earning it the colloquial name of "carpenter shark"). Although shark-like in appearance, it is in fact a skate, living on the ocean floor and using its rostrum to grub in the mud for crustaceans and other prey. Given its nocturnal habit and the murky conditions of its habitat, it's no surprise that the sawfish has poor eyesight; more surprising is that the rostrum is its primary sensory device, covered with tiny electro- and motion-sensitive pores that allow it to detect hidden prey by movement and even by its heartbeat. The rostrum may also be used to slash at passing prey in the water, usually stunning rather than killing, but rendering the object of its aggression easily overcome and consumed. This fine complementary pair make for strikingly aesthetic display pieces, in superb condition in light and dark creamy shades with a complete complement of "teeth" (in actuality, modified denticles), and mounted vertically on metal bases they stand 37¼ and 37½ inches high overall.
Estimate: $800-$1,100

49014 COMPLETE GIANT CLAM SHELL
Tridacna gigas
South Pacific

The Giant Clam is the largest living bivalve mollusk, inspiration for numerous lurid literary and cinematic adventure tales as a fatal trap for unwary divers and foolhardy pearl-hunters. It is native to the warm seas of the Indo-Pacific region and known traditionally to the Pacific Islanders as Pa'ua. The Pa'ua can grow up to 4 feet across and weigh over 440 lb, and they enjoy an average life span of 100 years or more, although they are entirely sessile in adulthood (meaning that they remain anchored to the seabed). Of an elegant, undulating form, the exterior of this present example displays an evocative rough ocean texture, and even sports the remains of the connective tissue that hinged the two halves of the shell in life; it is relatively rare to obtain both halves, and this is a fine-sized specimen weighing over 250 lb and measuring 33 inches across.
Estimate: $1,800-$2,400

49015   LARGE BUTTERFLY DISPLAY CASE
Various species
Peru

This dazzling display case contains 100 species of tropical butterflies and moths from ten separate families. It is a veritable feast for the eyes; a stunning demonstration of the huge variety in colors and patterns found on these delicate and beautiful insects; expertly mounted, they are presented in a mahogany case glazed on both sides to display just as much variety again on the underside of the wings. Both an invaluable guide to lepidoptery and a stunning display piece, it measures 25 x 34¾ inches.

Estimate: $1,800-$2,400

49016 LARGE BUTTERFLY SWARM DISPLAY
Morpho amathonte
Peru

The large *M.amathonte* is one of the most beautiful of all neo-tropical butterflies, as amply demonstrated by this large and impressive display case. Thirty-six specimens are expertly mounted in a swarming pattern, their electric blue wings shimmering with iridescence. The mahogany case is glazed on both sides to allow a perfect view of the completely contrasting underside, and in addition also allows light to pass through the delicate wings, creating a ghostly fusion of delicate blue, pale tan with eerie eye-shaped markings. A superb and striking display it measures 48 x 36 inches.

Estimate: $1,800-$2,400

49017 KAMMERERITE (CHROMIAN CLINOCHLORE)
*Kop Krom Mine, Kop Daglari, Erzurum Province,
Eastern Anatolia Region, Turkey*

It is truly unfortunate that fine Kammererite, also known as Chromian Clinochlore, is virtually a one locality mineral. All but one of the few localities for this exotic Chromian Mica, produce lackluster specimens that look like port wine stains on rock, even under a microscope. The sole exception is material from the Kop Krom Mine in Turkey, where the mineral appears as sharp and lustrous prisms that are the hue of young red wines. Greyish-black massive Chromite, the actual ore mineral sought, serves as the matrix for these delightfully brash specimens. It is also quite unfortunate that this mine is near the end of its productive lifespan. The supply of Kammererite has always been very limited and the situation is likely to get worse. This exceptional example is from the collection of the late Dr. Marvin Rausch, a well known collector who specialized in excellent quality specimens but with particular focus on cabinet to large cabinet sized pieces. The specimen bears his accession number 121. It was probably mined in the 1970's since that was when the best of the material hit the market. Larger, ¼ inch, di-pyramidal crystals are interspersed with smaller ones down to the micro level. They are evenly distributed over the front as well as the back of the specimen. The condition is fine, with a little minor nicking – not unexpected. This material, at this level of quality, is only going to become more collectible. It measures 3½ x 3½ x 1½ inches and has a custom labeled base.
Provenance: Marvin Rausch Collection
Estimate: $7,000-$9,000

49018 YELLOW & BLUE FLUORITE
*Minerva No. 1 Mine, Ozark-Mahoning Group,
Cave-in-Rock Sub-District, Illinois-Kentucky
Fluorspar District, Hardin Co., Illinois, USA*

Back in the 1980's, what appeared to be a never ending, steady flow of colorful, affordable and large Fluorite groups was coming from a mining district centered about Hardin County, Illinois, where it was being mined for the chemical industry. Literal tons of such material were mined and sold to collectors. Today, that river has run dry – the ore zones are mined out. Almost invariably, the only material seen is "B" grade or worse, and usually it is "aesthetically challenged" to be kind. The only time fine material becomes available is when a collection is dispersed. The best of the material mined is conceded to feature a yellow or golden central core overcoated with light blue or purple exterior layers. This specimen not only displays those features but in addition, it has a "phantom layer" of minute Chalcopyrite/Pyrite crystals dusting the interface between the yellow core and the blue outer layers. If that isn't enough, there are spherical hollows where a globular mineral, probably Barite, was dissolved away by natural solutions and some of those cavities, as well as the Fluorite exterior, are sprinkled with little "dog-tooth spar" Calcite twins. The main Fluorite cube measures 4 inches on edge and there are others nearly as large. Overall dimensions are 8¼ x 9 x 4½ inches and it is in excellent condition.
Provenance: Jim & Dawn Minette Collection
Estimate: $18,000-$22,500

49019 TWINNED FLUORITE WITH SPHALERITE ON GALENA

Elmwood Mine, Carthage, Central Tennessee
Ba-F-Pb-Zn District, Smith Co., Tennessee, USA

The Elmwood Mine near Carthage, Tennessee, was the home for a few hundred millenia for this delightful combination of three very different minerals. Most notable among them is a twinned lavender crystal of Fluorite liberally dusted with lustrous, reddish brown Sphalerite crystals all of which are located, as if by design, upon a metallic cube of Galena. The form of the Fluorite is stellate in cross-section with "fins" or arms radiating out along the "C" or long axis. The pale violet coloration possesses golden undertones that are visible when viewed from certain directions. Dusting the exterior of the Fluorite are discrete, isolated Sphalerite crystals of a deep reddish-brown hue; they are lustrous and almost metallic in reflection. The Galena cube has the "clipped corners" that are characteristic octahedral modifications common to some examples of this mineral. The Galena's luster is a dark, metallic one with a certain amount of intricate surface detail produced by complex growth features on the exterior. The overall specimen measures approximately 3½ x 2¼ x 1¼ inches. There is no base since the Galena functions very well as one. In pristine condition and from an old museum collection.
Estimate: $12,000-$15,000

49020 LILAC PURPLE FLUORITE CUBE PERCHED ON SPHALERITE

Elmwood Mine, Carthage, Central Tennessee
Ba-F-Pb-Zn District, Smith Co., Tennessee, USA

Closed now, the Elmwood Mine of Carthage, Tennessee, was a prolific producer of exquisite Fluorite on Sphalerite specimens for many years. The better examples from Elmwood are easily identifiable by their colorless transparency that grades into a light lilac. The simple cubic habit, with complex surface features, contrasts nicely with the dark and lustrous reddish brown of the Sphalerite group at the base of the specimen. There is a minor "ding" to one of the back corners and a minuscule amount of nicking to a front edge, otherwise excellent condition. Back side of specimen shows attachment point to fissure wall. On a custom labeled acrylic base, overall measurements are 3½ x 3⅜ x 2¾ inches.
Estimate: $3,200-$3,600

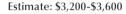

49021 HERKIMER "DIAMOND" CLUSTER

Herkimer Co., New York, USA

A classic group of "Herkimer Diamonds" from upstate New York, made up of 10 doubly-terminated Quartz crystals with brilliant luster and limpid transparency. Some of the stubby prisms contain black inclusions of "Anthraxolite:" a complex mixture of organic compounds that are thought partially responsible for this unusual occurrence of Quartz. The back side of the group show signs of its attachment to the walls of the local limestone. This bright, sculptural group displays a mere hint of smoky color; not unusual for this material. A few terminations show minor nicking, otherwise the condition is excellent. The group measures 3 x 2¾ x 1¼ inches and comes with a custom base.
Provenance: Ken Silvey Collection; Ed David Collection #64V
Estimate: $3,500-$4,500

49022 AMETHYST

Las Vigas Region, Veracruz, Mexico

The mountainous interior of the state of Veracruz in Mexico boasts one of the world's most renowned Amethyst sources: Las Vigas. The unique character of these violet gems is apparent in a number of ways. Unlike most Amethyst crystals which tend to be "stubby," the Las Vigas ones tend to be relatively long and narrow. In addition, they typically show a color zonation going from virtually colorless at the base to a clear medium purple at the termination. This specimen, studded with a profusion of Amethyst crystals, is a prime example of those traits along with excellent luster and great transparency. Some of the crystals are doubly-terminated and are up to 1⅜ inches in length. All rise from a typical matrix of grey-green volcanic rock. In pristine condition, it measures 8 inches high by 4½ inches wide by 2¾ inches deep and has a custom labeled base.

Estimate: $5,500-$6,500

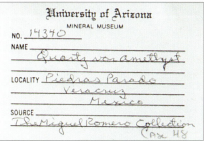

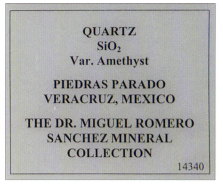

49023 QUARTZ (VAR. AMETHYST)

Piedra Parada, Mun. de Tatatila, Veracruz, Mexico

Limpid, lustrous and possessed of the kind of purple that small children instinctively want, there is no substitute for Veracruz Amethyst. It's not the darkest of shades, but there is something magical about the combination that speaks to the child in all of us. This specimen spoke to Dr. Miguel Romero Sanchez, late owner of what was arguably the finest collection of Mexican minerals in the world. It consists of several doubly-terminated prisms, up to 2 inches in length, of light violet hue joined together at their bases and sides, that are arranged by nature in a pleasing composition. There is no matrix, which is not unusual for this type of Amethyst. The luster is the brilliant type these specimens are noted for. The condition is excellent and the specimen is accompanied by a custom fitted base. It measures 2½ x 2¼ x 1 inch.

Provenance: University of Arizona; Romero Collection #14340

Estimate: $3,000-$3,500

49024   QUARTZ "V" (VAR. AMETHYST AND SMOKY)

Goboboseb Mountains, Brandberg area, Brandberg District, Erongo Region, Namibia
The Goboboseb locality, also mentioned in the next lot, has been known to infrequently produce odd combinations of the various types of Quartz. The "V" shaped crystal group seen here is a case in point. By all rights, both sides of this pair should display equal amounts of Amethyst and Smoky Quartz. That's not how it worked: one side has the lion's share of violet Amethyst while the other ended up with most of the Smoky Quartz. As if that wasn't enough to puzzle the observer, the forms of the "arms" are quite different as well. The Amethyst side, while doubly terminated, is still in essence a simple form of crystal. The Smoky side is a riotous conglomeration of: a Cathedral termination style, numerous "fensters" and considerable amounts of "phantom zones" thrown in for good measure. Pinpoint Hematite inclusions pepper both sides. The Smoky "arm" measures 3 inches long while the Amethyst side is a shorter 2⅜ inches from termination to termination. There is minor nicking, not unusual, otherwise in fine condition. Ex Charles Key and later the Marshall Sussman collection. Overall measurements are 3¼ x 2¼ x 1 inch and it has a custom base.
Estimate: $2,000-$2,500

49025   QUARTZ WITH AMETHYST PHANTOM AND WATER BUBBLES

Goboboseb Mountains, Brandberg area, Brandberg District, Erongo Region, Namibia
The drive to find and possess beautiful things is strong and sometimes leads to places far from any pretense of "civilization." The arid volcanic tableland of the Goboboseb Mountains in West Central Namibia is a prime example. Local miners brave fierce heat and the total absence of anything necessary for daily life: water, shelter & food – things we take for granted. All for a chance to pull a deep purple treasure from the shadowy depths of an ancient lava flow where it has quietly waited for more years than Man has lived on this planet. This exceptional Amethyst displays a number of the features that Goboboseb specimens are renowned for. The deep purple internal hue is tempered with reddish highlights and is enclosed within an outer layer of colorless Quartz exhibiting sparkling Hematite/Lepidocrocite inclusions just below the terminal faces. The luster is excellent: extremely glassy. The "bottom" surface shows signs of fracturing and regrowth while the crystal was growing; one could argue on that basis that the crystal is doubly terminated. As an lagniappe, there are moving bubbles trapped within the violet interior of the crystal: water trapped while the lava was still cooling and the crystal was still growing, thousands of millenia ago. This fine specimen measures 4½ x 1⅛ inches in diameter and sits on a custom base.
Provenance: Charles Key Collection
Estimate: $3,500-$4,500

49026   QUARTZ: AMETHYST SCEPTER

Jerome Street, Ashaway, Hopkinton, Washington Co., Rhode Island, USA
Like the blink of an eye, the production history of this locality was over before most collectors had even heard of it. The locality is now gone – that the locality was in a housing tract might have had something to do with it. In any event these very attractive Amethyst "scepter" crystals vanished into collections overnight. This excellently representative example features a well developed "head" of medium purple Amethyst with minor Smoky overtones, proudly capping a colorless Quartz prism with complex faces on the exterior. Low and to the side is a secondary prism that is devoid of Amethyst, but nevertheless serves to further illustrate the complex surface topology already mentioned. There is miniscule nicking to the back side of the termination, otherwise excellent condition. Overall dimensions are 2½ x 1⅜ x 1¼ inches and it has a custom labeled base.
Estimate: $3,500-$4,000

AMETHYST

Jacksons Crossroads, Wilkes Co., Georgia, USA

49027   AMETHYST "FLOWER" ON MATRIX

Wonderful things have come from an out of the way part of Georgia called Jacksons Crossroads. Here open pit mining operations have produced some of the finest North American Amethyst ever seen. The drop-dead luscious purple hue of this treasure is equaled by the brilliantly glassy luster and transparency. It also doesn't hurt for the Amethyst to take the form of a "flower" perched rather prominently upon a matrix of colorless Quartz "needles." The condition is pristine and the overall composition is stunning in its perfection. The specimen measures 4½ x 5 x 3¾ inches and comes with a custom labeled base.

Estimate: $40,000-$47,500

ELMWOOD CALCITE

Elmwood Mine, Carthage, Central Tennessee Ba-F-Pb-Zn District, Smith Co., Tennessee, USA

49028   CALCITE ON FLUORITE

Considering Mother Nature's extremely broad aesthetic, ranging all the way from warthogs on one end to specimens such as this on the other, it is tempting to assert that Nature was having a VERY good day when this treasure was fashioned. Attempts at anthropomorphicizing Nature are doomed to failure, however – Nature produces sublime works as well as ridiculous ones with the same lack of concern. That lack of concern led to a fortuitous combination of a warm golden orange, perfect Scalenohedral twin crystal of shining Calcite measuring 5½ to 6 inches long, artfully balanced upon a plinth of crystalline blue-violet Fluorite of cubic form. This is from the Helmut Bruckner Collection – Mr. Bruckner is a very well known German dealer and this is an old acquisition from his personal collection. It has a custom labeled base and measures 8¼ x 9 x 5½ inches.
Estimate: $120,000-$160,000

49029   CALCITE
Basalt Quarry, Ambariomiambana, Sambava Departement., Sava, (North-Eastern) Region, Ansiranana Province, Madagascar

Madagascar is a veritable treasure house of gems and minerals. With the exception of Diamonds, all of the other major gems are found there. So it's no surprise that the Calcite from this island may be special as well. This honey colored Calcite was mined from a Basalt quarry presumably operated for "road metal" as the crushed gravel used for road base is called. When the workers discovered shiny crystals in cavities, their cultural familiarity with mineral specimens kicked in and inquiries regarding potential value were made. This specimen has been held back by the miners since 2004. Besides the attractive and transparent color, the specimen exhibits an unusual form of twinning: something Calcite is famous for. Since the host rock is a volcanic one, it comes as no surprise that there are well crystallized and colorless Stilbite laths associated with the Calcite. A white area in the center seems to be either "contact" or where a Stilbite used to be. Condition otherwise is excellent, and the luster is glassy. With a custom labeled base, the sizable specimen measures a considerable 7 x 7 x 5 inches.
Estimate: $8,000-$10,000

49030   CLASSIC ENGLISH CALCITE
Egremont, West Cumberland Iron Field, North and Western Region, Cumbria, England

As an industrial mineral, Calcite is right up there with sand in terms of little value per ton. Nevertheless, old Cumberland English Calcite specimens (and they are ALL old) are held in high regard by collectors ever since Victorian gentlemen adopted mineral collecting as a proper sort of avocation. At that time, specimens such as this one were quite common and affordable. Now, the few that have survived, are fought over as "Classics" from another, more genteel, era. This matrix example displays the typical colorless transparency that Cumberland was famous for. The crystal "habit" is also quite characteristic of the material from Egremont in West Cumberland, showing an elongated prism and typical terminal faces as well. There are a multitude of crystals to 1¼ inches long thickly covering the dark brown matrix. Three are cleaved but from the normal viewing perspective they are on the backside and therefore; inconsequential, especially given the age of the piece. Accession #1168 is on the specimen, but there is no information as to whose collection that number was associated with. Possessing excellent luster, it measures 3¼ x 2¾ x 2 inches
Provenance: Harvard Museum via George Elling Collection
Estimate: $2,500-$3,000

49031 ETTRINGITE
N'Chwaning Mines, Kuruman, Kalahari Manganese Fields, Northern Cape Province, South Africa
The mineral collecting world was caught by surprise when the first Ettringite specimens from South Africa appeared. Previously known from other localities, the mineral, up to that point was, to be charitable ... aesthetically challenged. The new examples changed all that. Most were loose crystals without any matrix, making the specimen exhibited here one of the exceptional ones recovered. Yellow-green, stout hexagonal prisms up to ¾ of an inch long, sprout from a dark, irregular matrix liberally dusted with druzy micro-crystals, presumably Quartz. The Ettringite shows a certain amount of zoning when closely examined, with golden areas visible near the terminations. Condition is excellent, which is to be expected considering that the specimen is from the Jim & Dawn Minette collection. It measures 2⅜ x 2 x 1 inch.
Estimate: $4,500-$5,500

49032 HEMATITE & ETTRINGITE
N'Chwaning Mines, Kuruman, Kalahari Manganese Fields, Northern Cape Province, South Africa
The Manganese Mines of N'chwaning in South Africa have produced some very notable examples of Hematite as well as Ettringite over the last 20+ years or so. What they haven't produced to any degree are specimens combining the two. This is because Hematite forms on the ceiling of the cavities and Ettringite tends to form on the floor. Out of a recent find at the mine, there was only one that did combine the two minerals. This unique example is that one. The metallic black Hematite shows the form typical of a twinned crystal and has the mirror-bright luster that N'Chwaning is famous for. It is associated with smaller Hematite crystals decreasing in size all the way to microscopic ones. Several lemon-yellow prisms of Ettringite up to 1½ + inches in length, grace the side and back of the specimen. The most prominent one shows its double termination very clearly. Both of the minerals are in excellent condition. The specimen measures 5 x 3 x 2½ inches overall and it has a custom labeled base.
Estimate: $40,000-$50,000

49033 SMITHSONITE

Kelly Mine, Magdalena District, Socorro Co., New Mexico, USA

If you ask a seasoned mineral collector, "Where does the best Smithsonite come from?," chances are the material from the Kelly Mine in New Mexico will be in the top three and that's being conservative. There are the smooth, almost feminine curves and a translucent green-blue color that fine Jade wishes it possessed, and then there's the unique luster that isn't shiny and isn't matte, but is complexly captivating. The sum total of aesthetic qualities shown by this mineral is enough to captivate anyone, from the rankest amateur to the museum curator who's seen it all. Here, an exposed cavity on one side allows a glimpse into the normally hidden interior of this wondrous glowing gem. There, fine acicular bladed crystals of Aurichalcite can be seen in the depths of the hollow area, low and to one side of the specimen. This is normally seen only on broken edges and is considered quite unusual. The Aurichalcite has been overcoated with translucent blue-green Smithsonite giving even more apparent depth to the piece. The satiny luster is accented by a small group of druzy Calcite crystals perched upon the "shoulder" of the specimen – again quite unusual for this locality. The specimen measures 3 x 2 x 1 inch, is in excellent condition and has a custom base.

Provenance: Larry Conklin Collection

Estimate: $5,000-$6,000

49034   BRIGHT YELLOW SMITHSONITE

Masua Mine, Masua, Iglesias, Carbonia-Iglesias Province, Sardinia, Italy

Traces of Cadmium substituting for Zinc in the crystal structure account for the bright yellow coloration of this classic Smithsonite from the island of Sardinia. Yellow is one of the more desirable of color variants of Smithsonite. Besides the unusual color, the specimen gets extra points for the classic botryoidal habit and unique luster that Smithsonite possesses. The piece is from the famous Minette Collection, with labels to match, and is featured in the recent mineralogical magazine "Smithsonite, Think Zinc!," page 26. The accession number S-134 on the base of specimen matches the Minette labels but the specimen itself dates to the 1800's. A rare specimen, as most of this material was used as lapidary material. With exceptional provenance, it measures 5½ inches high by 3½ inches wide by 3¼ inches thick, is in fine condition and has a custom base.

Provenance: Minette Collection

Estimate: $30,000-$40,000

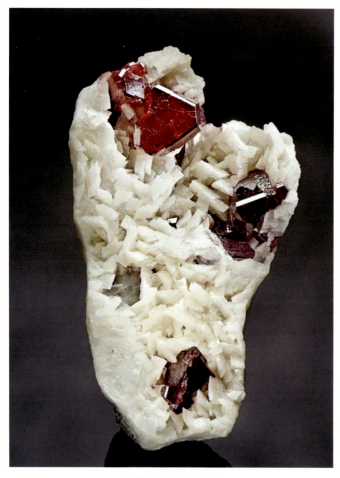

49035   CINNABAR

Yunchangping Mine, Wanshan District, Tongren Prefecture, Guizhou Province, People's Republic of China

Chinese Cinnabars have set the standard for this mineral on a worldwide basis. The reason for this is fairly straightforward: in size, perfection and sheer variety of forms, the Chinese material has no equal. Unusually light in color and possessing excellent transparency, this group of pseudo-pyramidal crystals is nestled amongst contrasting white and cream colored Dolomite crystals with a colorless Quartz prism thrown in as a *lagniappe*. The luster is the almost metallic one common to high R.I. minerals and gems. With increasing internal Chinese demand, fine crystal groups such as this are appearing less and less frequently on the international market: a situation not likely to improve in the future. The largest crystal is aproximately ½ inch across and the specimen measures 3 x 1¾ x 1 inches. From the Steve and Clara Smale collection, it is in pristine condition and comes with a custom labeled base.

Provenance: Steve and Clara Smale collection
Estimate: $5,500-$6,500

49036   BLUE SPINEL

Ganesh, Hunza Valley, Gilgit District, Northern Areas, Pakistan

Since colored Spinel is a highly desirable gemstone, it is no wonder that it is also in high demand as a mineral specimen. Of all the colors found, a pure Sapphire-blue is one of the rarest.

In addition to its pure blue coloration, this lovely specimen displays a very well-developed octahedral crystal form; again, not common. The sharp, blue octahedrons have been exposed by the careful, mechanical removal of the white Marble matrix; a tedious and delicate task at best. Additionally, the mountain heights of Ganesh in the Hunza Valley of Pakistan are the home of this sky blue wonder, which is not an easy place to mine or stay alive in. All of these things contribute to there not being a large or constant supply of such blue Spinel. The largest crystal is ⅝ inch across and there are two additional crystals emerging from the Marble matrix. Overall measurements are 2½ x 1⅛ x 1¹⁄₁₆ inches, it has a custom labeled base and is in excellent condition.

Estimate: $1,500-$1,800

49037   FLUORAPOPHYLLITE ON STILBITE

Momin Akhada, Rahuri, Ahmadnagar District, Maharashtra, India

Although Apophyllite occurs with considerable regularity across the Deccan Plateau of India, there is only one locality there that produces these distinctively spherically radiating aggregates of pale green Apophyllite with the flat terminations. Discovered fairly recently, this variety rapidly shot to the top of the pile in the world market. Good specimens command premium prices among today's collectors. Found in 2001, the example seen here features the characteristic, pale mint-green globular Apophyllite clusters up to 1¾ inches in diameter, randomly distributed over a matrix of cream colored Stilbite. As is typical for this material, the luster is glassy and the crystals are sharply defined. The condition is excellent and the rather large specimen measures 10 x 10 x 5½ inches high.

Estimate: $5,000-$6,000

49038   CAVANSITE
*Wagholi Quarry, Wagholi, Pune District
(Poonah District), Maharashtra, India*

It is the ignoble fate of Cavansite to be simultaneously one of the most desirable members of the mineral kingdom and yet suffer from the boredom of easily jaded collectors who unconsciously feel that the supply of Cavansite is, like Diamond, forever. Not true, as anyone with a sense for probability and history can see. This is, for all practical purposes, a one locality mineral and when that modest little locality becomes a housing tract instead of a small quarry, then the supply is *finie*. Fine examples, of which this is one, will garner considerable "coulda, woulda, shoulda" commentary by those who failed to grasp the supply side economics involved.

This matrix specimen possesses the prime requirements for a fine Cavansite specimen. It is a group of several (6+) spherical aggregates of deep teal-blue Cavansite crystals perched artfully upon a typical matrix of tiny, colorless Stilbite laths with a larger Stilbite crystal thrown in for good measure. The largest sphere spans some 1¹⁄₁₆ inches in diameter; quite sizable for this mineral. Beneath the crust of Stilbite lies the dark basaltic lava that provided the proper conditions for the Cavansites growth and protection. There is an indication that there was another spherical group on the back of the main aggregate, otherwise in excellent condition. With a custom base, overall measurements are 4 x 3 x 2 inches.

Estimate: $5,000-$6,000

49039   ORPIMENT
Twin Creeks Mine, Potosi District, Humboldt Co., Nevada, USA

Orpiment is a mineral with a very old linkage with humankind: the name is derived from the Latin word "Auripigmentum," meaning "Golden Pigment," a clear indication of its use in ancient times. Being a sulfide of the dreaded element Arsenic, one would think that this utilization would be short-lived. Not so, since Arsenic, in the sulfide form as Orpiment, is remarkably insoluble and therefore quite inoffensive under normal conditions. The beautiful golden tint possessed by Orpiment is quite unique among minerals, perhaps shared only by Gold, the mineral that the miners were really seeking. This Orpiment was an accidental by-product of Newmont Mining's Twin Creeks Gold Mine in Nevada. It was taken out a number of years ago and more specimens are not likely to be forthcoming. The largest crystal is approximately ⅝ of an inch across and there are numerous crystals of similar dimensions covering the rest of the specimen. In fine condition, this warm golden piece of history measures 2¾ x 2½ x 1¾ inches and comes with a custom labeled base.

Estimate: $5,000-$6,000

AZURITE

Milpillas Mine, Cuitaca, Mun. de Cananea, Sonora, Mexico

49040   AZURITE CRYSTALS

From a recent find in Sonora, Mexico, comes this brilliantly lustrous group of large Azurite blades, some of which are partially altered to chatoyant, green Malachite. The Azurite crystals cement fragments of a grey limestone that occupied portions of an open fissure in the ore body. Other than obvious attachment points to the walls of the fissure, these sizable crystals are sharp, complete and undamaged. The largest of them measures an impressive 1¾ inches in length. Overall dimensions of this large cabinet specimen are 9 inches high by 3½ inches wide by 3 inches thick. The largest and finest specimen from a small pocket found in 2008, it is in pristine condition and has a custom base.

Estimate: $140,000-$180,000

49041 CLASSIC BISBEE AZURITE "VUG"

Bisbee, Warren District, Mule Mountains,
Cochise Co., Arizona, USA

Photographs of mining operations in Bisbee, Arizona, from the turn of the century (not this one – the one before) often show caverns lined with Azurite of every possible form, even stalactites. That they were beautiful in their perfection did not protect them from being turned into wire, coin and the like. The most attractive material was found close to the surface and was the first to go. Some of the miners thought to save an occasional piece from that destruction, which is why examples, such as this, exist. "Classic" Bisbee specimens display a mix of form and color saturation. That is the case here: the interior surfaces vary from a velvety, matte type to sparkling druze, which flash pinpoint reflections from hundreds of tiny crystal faces. Color also varies widely from a light powder blue all the way to deep Indigo in the druzy areas. The "Vug," or "Vugh" as the old-timers would spell it, shows the typical ocher Bisbee matrix with splashes of green Malachite on sides and back. In excellent condition, particularly for such a classic that is at least 100 years old. It measures 7 inches wide by 5½ inches tall by 6 inches deep and has a custom base.
Provenance: Marc Weill Collection

Estimate: $25,000-$35,000

49042 DEEP BLUE AZURITE

Touissit, Touissit District, Oujda-Angad
Province, Oriental Region, Morocco

Mines, like people, have their ups and downs when it comes to producing profits or interesting specimens. In many cases, mines still operating may no longer produce the same kind of specimens that they did in their heyday. This is a concrete example: while modern Moroccan Azurites are justifiably famous, the fine, bladed crystals in this specimen have not been produced for many, many years. It definitely dates from long before the 1970's – when the Howard Belsky collection was started. Spherical crystal aggregates of deep-blue, sub-parallel blades of Azurite cover the velvety green Malachite matrix. These aggregates range in size up to 1½ inches in diameter and they have occasional, contrasting, patches of bright green Malachite alteration. This a very fine and large specimen for the locality; it is from the personal collection of the late Howard Belsky, mineral collector and dealer. This Old Classic displays excellent luster and condition and would be a worthy addition to any collectors cabinet. It measures 7 x 5 x 2 inches thick and has a custom acrylic base.
Provenance: Howard Belsky Collection

Estimate: $16,000-$19,000

49043 ROBIN'S EGG BLUE CHRYSOCOLLA WITH GREEN MALACHITE "EYES"

Kamoto Principal Mine, Kamoto, Kolwezi, Western area, Katanga Copper Crescent, Katanga (Shaba), Democratic Republic of Congo (Zaïre)

The "bull's-eye" pattern shown by the polished areas of this natural artwork are the result of a cooperative effort between Mother Nature and a lapidary artist: Mother Nature provided spherical, green Malachite crystal groups overcoated by turquoise-blue Chrysocolla and the lapidary artist provided the skill necessary to cut through the Chrysocolla, exposing the green interiors of the rounded aggregates. A final, bright polish completes the artistic collaboration. This colorful sculpture measures 6 inches high by 6 inches wide and is 3 inches thick. It stands upright on its sawn base.

Estimate: $1,200-$1,500

49044 PRIMARY MALACHITE CRYSTAL

Mashamba West Mine, Kolwezi, Western area, Katanga Copper Crescent, Katanga (Shaba), Democratic Republic of Congo (Zaïre)

Malachite appears in two variants: Primary and Secondary. Primary Malachite is the form deposited by copper rich hydrothermal fluids as they ascend from deep in the Earth from their magmatic source rocks. Secondary Malachite is a product of near-surface copper minerals being attacked by oxygenated rainwater percolating downward, going into solution and further down, redeposited as the solutions are neutralized by reactions with the host rock. The greatest percentage of the Malachite mined is Secondary in nature. The relevance of this difference is that Primary Malachite forms much larger crystals in general than the Secondary variety. Here we have curved aggregates of blocky crystals uniting to form crystal "rosettes." Two groups of crystals interpenetrate giving the entire specimen a cross type of form. That this is an older Congo specimen is attested to by its having been handled by Gilbert Gauthier, Belgian mining engineer and dealer from some years back. Subsequently it has resided in the collection of Dr. Ed David, Science & Technology Advisor to President Nixon. It measures 2⅛ x 2 x 1¾ inches and is in fine condition, with only very minor wear on some edges.

Provenance: Ed David Collection

Estimate: $1,500-$1,800

49045   DRUZY MALACHITE OVER MALACHITE — NATURAL VUG

L'Etoile de Congo Mine, Katanga Province, Congo

Very sparkly areas of druzy Malachite overcoat pale turquoise-blue, botryoidal aggregates of Chrysocolla on the front of this cave-like specimen. It is difficult to conceive that ground water, slowly percolating downward through a mass of Copper enriched rock, could create the "Easter Egg" display seen here. In fine condition, it sits on a custom labeled base and measures 7½ inches high by 5½ inches wide by 3 inches deep.
Estimate: $2,500-$3,500

49046   AZURE BLUE CORNETITE

L'Etoile de Congo Mine, Katanga Province, Congo

Copper minerals, of which this is one, often tend to exhibit various shades of blue and green coloration. Subtle differences in those colors allow collectors to differentiate between the various minerals on sight. Cornetite: a rare Copper Phosphate from the Congo is one that is sufficiently different in form and color to be identifiable by sight alone. The surfaces tend to be made up of thousands of tiny, sparkling crystals arranged like cumulus clouds in rounded, billowing masses. Their color ranges from almost black to a dark teal blue that, once seen, is difficult to forget. All surfaces other than the base, are liberally coated with these scintillating little "points of light," even the back side. In fine condition, other than a few minor nicks, it measures 5¼ inches high by 3⅝ inches wide by 2 inches thick and sits in a custom labeled base.
Estimate: $6,000-$7,000

49047 DIOPTASE

Tsumeb Mine (Tsumcorp Mine), Tsumeb, Otjikoto (Oshikoto) Region, Namibia

Mineral collectors and curators may not agree on much, but one thing they do tend to agree upon is the place of fine Tsumeb Dioptase specimens in the desirability rankings of such people. Specimens like this one are, if not at the top of the list, they are very, very close to it. Why? The short form is the color: color so unearthly that cameras and film and the like, literally cannot capture an exact representation of it. What can be captured, as has been here, is the overall form, composition and luster of this large and exquisite example. Individual crystals up to ½ inch liberally cover the light colored limestone matrix of the specimen. Any imperfections in the Dioptase are confined to the edges of the piece where it was broken free from the surrounding rock. The luster of the Dioptase is glassy, as only exhibited by the very best material. This very sizable cabinet specimen measures 6 x 4 x 3 inches, is in excellent condition and has a custom labeled base.

Provenance: Marc Weil Collection; Stuart Wilensky Collection

Estimate: $85,000-$100,000

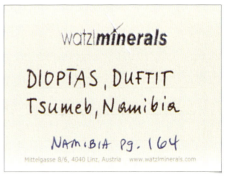

49048   DIOPTASE WITH DUFTITE

Tsumeb Mine, Tsumeb, Otjikoto Region, Namibia

Fine Tsumeb specimens do not normally present viewers with mineralogical puzzles – the combination of Dioptase, Duftite and Calcite is usually straight-forward in nature. What is odd about this example, is that **this** specimen, pictured and described in the book "Namibia" by von Bezing (p. 164) is identified as being "Dioptase on Duftite coated Calcite." Close examination of the form of the "Calcite" under the coatings, raises the question of whether the actual sequence is an anomalous one of: Large Dioptase xtls forming on matrix, overcoating of everything with a mixed Calcite/Duftite druze, and finally a secondary deposition of Dioptase on top of everything. Whichever is the case, this is a very unusual example of Dioptase from this most unusual mine. The underlying Dioptase crystals range in size up tp ⅝ of an inch while the paper thin secondary ones are approximately ¼ or ⁵⁄₁₆ of an inch. Condition is pristine and there is a custom base for this most unique specimen that measures 3 x 3 x 2⅝ inches.

Estimate: $14,000-$18,000

49049 DIOPTASE

La Farola Mine, Cerro Pintado, Las Pintadas District, Tierra Amarilla, Copiapó Province, Atacama Region, Chile

For as many exotic and aesthetic minerals as Chile is home to, it is surprising how few are seen on the market. In any event, one of the rare minerals that Chile is known for, is the seldom seen Chilean Dioptase. This example is quite representative of the material from the Mina La Farola, home to a number of interesting minerals. The Dioptase is presented as a druzy, micro-crystalline layer, partially overcoated with what appears to be druzy Quartz. There are areas that appear to host minor amounts of Aurichalcite, another copper mineral rarely found in association with Dioptase. The golden-brown, banded matrix shows through the Dioptase at several attachment/contact points, otherwise the blue-green coating uniformly covers the front and top side of the specimen. Condition is very fine for this locality, especially given the size of the specimen, which measures 5 x 4 x 1¾ inches.

Estimate: $1,700-$2,000

49050   AMAZONITE & SMOKY QUARTZ

Smoky Hawk Claim, Teller Co., Colorado

Considerable quantities of the colorful variety of Microcline called Amazonite have emanated from Colorado as well as a number of other worldwide locations over the years. What was never available in significant quantity is the combination of Amazonite and Smoky Quartz, especially in undamaged condition. Ground movement and pocket collapse have destroyed more potentially fine specimens than all of the hamhanded collectors on the planet a hundred times over. As a direct result, a specimen like this, showing fine Amazonite and Quartz crystals with intact terminations is a rarity. There are two main Smoky Quartz crystals, the largest one measures 3½ inches in length. Both are in excellent condition. There are over ten Amazonite prisms making up the matrix for the Quartz. All of them display the deep turquoise color of top end material and some of them show the colorless zoning of specific prism faces that appear from time to time. Their luster is as fine as any Amazonite in any collection known at this time. The underside has been stabilized to preclude separation between the Amazonite crystals as a simple precaution. Overall measurements for this fine specimen are 4½ x 3¾ x 4 inches.

Provenance: Stuart Wilensky collection

Estimate: $37,500-$45,000

TOURMALINE

Paprok, Nuristan Province, Afghanistan

49051   TOURMALINE AND SMOKY QUARTZ

The rainbow tinted Tourmalines of Afghanistan are justly famous as objects of almost religious appreciation. Upping the ante by a considerable amount is the much less frequently seen combination of fine Afghani Tourmaline with sharp and lustrous Smoky Quartz. Not that Quartz isn't a frequent associate of Tourmaline, it is – but most of it is pale or damaged and doesn't hold up its end of the aesthetic union. Here is a pair of Smoky Quartz crystals 14 cm (5½ inches) long that would be quite desirable in their own right, flanking gemmy and lustrous Tourmaline prisms bearing three distinct color bands: pink, green and back to pink at the terminations. The Tourmaline is 13 cm (5+ inches) long from base to tip and 2.5 cm (1 inch) in diameter. Nestled low and to the side of the Tourmaline, is a violet hued group of pearly Lepidolite crystals. Quite a combination for one specimen and one, rarely seen in such excellent condition. The group measures 6 x 4½ x 3 inches overall and has a custom labeled base.

Estimate: $120,000-$150,000

RUBELLITE

Jonas Mine, Conselheiro Pena, Doce Valley, Minas Gerais, Southeast Region, Brazil

49052 RUBELLITE TOURMALINE

Miners at the Jonas Mine in Brazil were stunned when in April of 1978; they encountered an enormous "pocket" deep in the mine. For Jonas Lima, it was literally the find of a lifetime, since there was only one discovery like this: nothing since has come close. Specimens from this pocket consistently show a distinctive cranberry red tint and are often associated with large bladed crystals of Clevelandite feldspar. This specimen is a prime example of that type. It was owned by family friends of Sr. Lima up until very recently and otherwise has not been shown. Large for even a Jonas specimen, it features numerous terminated Tourmaline prisms extending in size up to 6 cm (2+ inches) in diameter and 6+ cm in length. Snowy white Clevelandite blades several inches in length are intermixed with the Tourmaline and occasional violet groups of Lepidolite Mica. Jonas specimens are always in high demand and large ones in excellent condition, even more so. The gorgeously colorful specimen measures approximately 15 x 15 x 5 inches and comes with a custom base. A piece of mineral collecting history not likely to be repeated any time soon.
Estimate: $85,000-$100,000

BLUE TOURMALINE

Paprok, Nuristan Province, Afghanistan

49053   BLUE TOURMALINE WITH RED TOP

Most things on the planet, people included, seem to come with a predictable level of imperfections. This makes it sometime a bit unnerving to find an object that appears to be designed and produced by Angels. Everything about this pastel treasure whispers "I am a mystery without limits." From the delicately bladed Clevelandite "sea foam" breaking around the massive, blue Tourmaline tower rising out of the waves, to the planar simplicity of the terminal face – everything about this treasure plays off complexity against simplicity, blue solidity against the merest, delicate thin line of red capping the last few millimeters, pale lavender Lepidolite nestled in the depths of the Clevelandite "breakers." This sublime art work has traveled halfway around the World to bring us the lesson that, whatever we do, Nature can do better and without needing our adulation or caring about our human concerns. This artless object measures a very significant 4½ x 4 x 4½ inches and has a custom labeled base. It is in pristine condition. One is not the owner of something like this; one is merely the caretaker, or the student.

Estimate: $55,000-$65,000

49054 ERYTHRITE

Bou Azzer, Bou Azzer District, Tazenakht, Ouarzazate Province, Souss-Massa-Draâ Region, Morocco

Cobalt, the element chiefly responsible for the dark magenta tint seen in this specimen, has a long and checkered history associated with it. European miners ascribed supernatural properties to ores containing it, chiefly because they looked like Silver ore but didn't contain any: bad joke on the miners. This was seen as the work of capricious mine spirits called Kobolds, hence the name Cobalt. There are no evil spirits hanging around this beautiful example of crystallized Erythrite: the Arsenate of Cobalt. Crystals of any size of this mineral are rarely seen in Cobalt mines, which make the veritable forest of Erythrite covering the top surface of this Moroccan specimen very desirable. Crystals up to 1 inch in length explode from the limonitic matrix in random directions, displaying textbook sub-parallel form and glassy luster. Most Moroccan samples of this mineral are damaged by rough handling, but this remarkable specimen has been spared such abuse. Its condition is superbly well-preserved, this exceptional specimen measures 3 x 3 x 2 inches and has a custom labeled base.

Estimate: $35,000-$45,000

49055   PYROMORPHITE

Daoping Mine, Gongcheng Co., Guilin Prefecture, Guangxi Zhuang Autonomous Region, China

Few minerals can compete with a fine Pyromorphite for attractiveness of form and brilliant color. The most desirable examples display a bright, almost fluorescent green coloration unique to the species. Setting the standard for such eye-catching wonders are the best of the Chinese Pyromorphites from the Daoping mine near Guilin – this fine specimen has lustrous, lime-green hexagonal prisms up to ½ inch in length coating the ceiling, walls and floor of this miniature "cave." The specimen shows a refreshing lack of damage – an imperfection that is all too common with most Pyromorphites. To keep the eye entertained, hints of an orange-brown gossan matrix peek out from the bottom and back side of this specimen. It measures 2¾ x 2½ x 2¼ inches and sits on a custom labeled base.

Estimate: $9,500-$11,000

49056 WULFENITE

Ojuela Mine, Mapimí, Mun. de Mapimí, Durango, Mexico

Known and worked from the times of the Spanish Conquest, the Ojuela Mine continues to amaze miners and collectors alike with the variety and excellence of mineral specimens wrested from its labyrinthine depths. No living individuals can know all of the hundreds of kilometers of passages that make up the mine. Wulfenite, an ore of Molybdenum and Lead, can be found in wonderfully crystallized examples showing exceptionally fine form and color. This specimen displays an elongated habit that is considerably rarer than the flat, tabular one normally seen. In addition, the golden yellow color and fine luster make this a choice addition to any collectors cabinet. In excellent condition, this large specimen measures 7 x 5 x 2 inches and sits in a custom labeled base.

Estimate: $5,000-$6,000

SULFUR 1929.
Cozzodosi Mine
Casteltermini, Agregento
Sicily, Italy

FROM THE COLLECTION OF
JACK HALPERN SAN FRANCISCO, CALIFORNIA

49057 EXCEPTIONAL SULFUR

Cozzodisi Mine, Casteltermini, Agrigento Province, Sicily, Italy

Sulfur & Brimstone – one of the foundations of Ancient as well as Modern industrial chemistry, without which life, as we know it, would be impossible. No Sulfur – no tires, fertilizer, modern paper, car batteries, matches and a host of other products we've all come to depend upon. For hundreds, perhaps thousands, of years the volcanic island of Sicily has provided the Mediterranean world with wine, olives, cheese and ... Sulfur. Labyrinthine passages, hewn by hand, honeycomb the rocks of the island. Sulfur from these deposits was mined, melted and cast into portable chunks for trade wherever merchant ships of the area traveled. All of which came to a crashing halt around 1900 when the Frasch Process proved to be more economical, slowly choking the Sicilian Sulfur mining industry to death. During that slow decline, miners supplemented their income by carefully saving the occasional, well crystallized specimen they encountered as they dug the raw Sulfur. The earliest date associated with this specimen is August 1972, as mentioned on an accompanying label from the Mineralogical Museum of Caltanissetta, indicating that the specimen had to have been mined prior to that. The specimen consists of a large group of bright yellow crystals on a minor colorless matrix of Calcite or Aragonite. The largest crystal is approximately 1½ inches across and all of them are transparent. The crystallization is sharp and the condition is excellent. With excellent provenance, it is from the award winning Jack Halpern Collection and measures 4½ x 3¾ x 2½ inches.

Estimate: $12,000-$15,000

49058 H-FL-APATITE ON FELDSPAR

Sapo Mine, Conselheiro Pena, Doce Valley, Minas Gerais, Southeast Region, Brazil

Apatite is one mineral that all of us have an intimate relationship with: our teeth and bone structure would have the structural strength of wet cardboard were it not for the wondrous combination of collagen and Apatite. Apatite also appears in beautiful and often colorful crystals as a result of simple inorganic processes in Nature. Here we have a host of tabular Apatite crystals up to 1¾ inches in length, of a medium green hue, scattered over the exterior of a Felspar mass. The material was part of a single find in 2004 at the Sapo Mine; a property previously known for beautiful, multicolored Tourmalines. The satiny luster obscures the transparent nature of the Apatite, but the cream color of the matrix Feldspar is visible through the Apatite wherever the matrix is in close contact. The Feldspar matrix itself exhibits a multitude of sharp crystal faces, providing a bit of textural variation. Considered from a chemical perspective, these Apatites are, strictly speaking, Hydroxyl-Fluoro-Apatite, a rather odd mix of additional elements that have taken up residence within the Apatite crystal lattice. As Apatite specimens go, this is a choice example based on: color, luster, crystal form, freedom from damage and excellent composition. It is in pristine condition and measures approximately 4 x 5¾ x 2 inches. There is no base, nor is one needed, as the specimen sits just fine on its own.

Estimate: $3,500-$4,000

49059   SODALITE (VAR. HACKMANITE)

Koksha Valley (Kokscha; Kokcha), Badakhshan (Badakshan; Badahsan) Province, Afghanistan

We tend to think of rocks and minerals as being dependably static. It's no accident that English is filled with mineral metaphors: Rock Solid, Rock of Ages, Rock Bottom, etc. It would appear that Hackmanite's major purpose is to challenge that view. This exotic variety of Sodalite displays the engaging property of changing color reversibly from colorless to a wild fuchsia-purple after exposure to Ultra-Violet Light. Exposure to daylight causes the color to fade away. The effect can be repeated indefinitely, but is destroyed by heating. Mineralogists refer to this as "tenebrescence" or reversible photochromism. This rather large matrix specimen features 3+ crystals, the largest measuring some 2 inches across, sitting on an off-white matrix. It is from a locality very close to the classic one for Lapis Lazuli in Afghanistan. The stout crystals are in fine condition with the typical glassy luster. An interesting example of a unique phenomenon that measures 6¼ x 3¼ x 2¾ inches.

Estimate: $4,000-$4,750

RHODONITE

Morro da Mina Mine, Conselheiro Lafaiete (old Queluz de Minas), Minas Gerais, Southeast Region, Brazil

49060   RHODONITE CRYSTALS

Rhodonite ($MnSiO_3$) is a Manganese ore that is very rarely encountered as crystals, even more so as the large and perfectly formed example seen here. This piece was the single, best specimen mined from a Brazilian "crystal cave". It has four sharp and lustrous crystals, ranging in size up to a very respectable 3 inches. Close examination reveals that all four are aligned in a parallel fashion indicating that the specimen is really a single very large crystal, five inches across, with multiple terminations! Crystals of this size and perfection are almost never offered for public sale. The color is a deep cherry red, on the edge of being pink, and it measures 5 x 2¾ x 1½ inches. The condition is excellent with great form, luster and luscious color. It has a custom acrylic base.
Estimate: $100,000-$140,000

TOPAZ

Minas Gerais, Brazil

49061   NATURAL BLUE TOPAZ

The discovery that Topaz can be irradiated, thereby imparting a beautiful, permanent blue color to otherwise colorless material, has had enormous impact on the colored gemstone trade. Not accidentally, the same process has called into question whether any given specimen of blue Topaz may also have been "treated." This is why older Topaz specimens, such as this one, are valued more highly for the simple reason that their known existence predates the development of that process and therefore their coloration is natural. The lovely color of this Brazilian gem crystal is an aesthetic complement to the very complex crystal habit that it displays: A myriad of sharply limned faces capture the eye and invite extended contemplation of Nature's talent for creative perfection. The largely gemmy crystal exhibits the classic flat termination, but with a twist: what would normally be a smooth plane is here a surface raven by a crevasse plunging into the icy blue heart of this frozen sculpture. The condition of this cool treasure can only be described as pristine. A minor amount of shimmering mica adorns the base, but that is the extent of any hint of matrix or other minerals. It measures 3½ x 4 x 3½ inches and comes with a custom labeled base.
Estimate: $22,000-$26,000

TANZANITE

Merelani Hills, Lelatema Mts, Arusha Region, Tanzania

49062   TANZANITE

Most owners of gem Tanzanite have never seen untreated material; the miners and cutters of Tanzanite routinely heat the rough material to suppress one of the three colors that this gemstone naturally displays. Even uncut gem crystals are heated to "improve" them. As a result, very few gem crystals show their natural coloration. This gem double crystal is the exception. Viewing from any one of the three possible directions produces startlingly different results: under incandescent light, one axis shows deep purple with reddish highlights, the second axis shows a sapphire blue and the third axis displays a deep pinkish-orange-red hue that is quite unexpected. Besides the wonderful palette of colors in transmitted light, there are further interactions between: the inclusions, the glassy surface luster and the numerous planar crystal faces – all of which combine to keep the eye captivated for hours. The crystal is quite gemmy and several stones could be cut from it, but that would be like melting down a 1933 Gold Double Eagle for bullion value. This rare and exotic gem treasure measures a very respectable 2½ x 1¾ x ⅞ inches and it proudly stands on a custom labeled base.

Estimate: $65,000-$75,000

EMERALD

North America Emerald Mines (formerly the Rist Mine), Hiddenite, Alexander Co., North Carolina, USA

49063   THE HILL TWIN EMERALD — LONGEST NORTH AMERICAN EMERALD CRYSTAL

That Emerald crystals could be found in the vicinity of Hiddenite, North Carolina, is well documented with discoveries going back to the 1800's. Such a possibility induced a local man to try his hand at Emerald mining. That man, James K. Hill Jr., has indicated that intuition played a major part in his decision to commence digging at a particular spot on his family's property in North Carolina in 1998. Twelve feet below the starting point of his new dig, he struck a cavity or "pocket," as they are called. Inside that pocket he found a pirate's treasure of Emerald crystals: some 3,300 carats of them to be exact. In the years since then, several other pockets were opened after Ground Penetrating Radar (GPR) indicated further potentially interesting targets. On August 23, 2006, one of those targets produced this specimen; the current record holder for longest North American Emerald known at 9½ inches! Due to a second Emerald crystal being attached to one side, it was christened "The Hill Twin Emerald." For a period it was held in the collection of NAEM (North American Emerald Mines), Mr. Hill's company, before entering the collection of Richard Geiger. In appearance, it is considerably longer than other Emeralds from this area, but other than that, it is quite representative of the North Carolina material. The coloration varies from almost colorless near the base and back, through a light "Emerald Green" over most of its length, darkening to a vibrant, gemmy green at the termination. The secondary crystal growing out from the side measures a significant 7¼ inches in length: very impressive in its own right. The secondary crystal also possesses a deeper color termination, albeit of smaller size. The basal section appears to be partially hollow for a short distance, which is in accord with the partial re-solution seen on that end. Supposedly found in three pieces in the pocket, whatever restorations have been done to it are quite invisible to the trained eye. Luster varies from muted at the base to glassy at the termination. The condition is excellent with the exception of the alleged restoration. Overall dimensions are 9½ inches long by 1⅛ inches at widest point by ½ inch wide at termination. This significant specimen, worthy of any museum collection, weighs a hefty 591 carats and comes with a custom base.
Estimate: $130,000-$150,000

49064   SAPPHIRE CRYSTAL
Sri Lanka

Any Sapphire crystal showing the least hint of transparency is immediately in danger of being cut into a gemstone. This is one reason (other than simple rarity) that decent Sapphire crystals are very infrequently seen in mineral collections. The particular specimen seen here carries the distinction of being featured among the award winning special display of connoisseur thumbnail specimens exhibited at the Tucson Gem & Mineral Show in 2010. The overall form of the crystal is a hexagonal shape in cross-section that tapers to a point at each end: a classic textbook example. Color varies from colorless to zones of light powder blue, especially near the terminations. It is quite transparent and shows fine luster with typical tiny striations on its crystal faces. There are a couple of minor secondary crystals and two brown inclusions of unknown composition. This euhedral crystal measures a respectable 1⅜ inches long by ½ inch by ⅜ of an inch and is in excellent condition.

Estimate: $6,000-$7,000

49065   SCHORL TOURMALINE, TOPAZ, AND CLEVELANDITE
Dassu, Shigar Valley, North of Skardu, Pakistan

Schorl is a variety of tourmaline that is black in color, and while it accounts for 95% of all tourmalines, aesthetic specimens such as the present one are difficult to find. Even rarer is to find a specimen in association with other gem minerals. The sherry topaz crystal and white clevelandite cluster are in perfect aesthetic contrast to the jet black tourmaline, making this an interesting association specimen. The overall specimen measures 2 x 2 x 1¼ inches.

Estimate: $1,100-$1,400

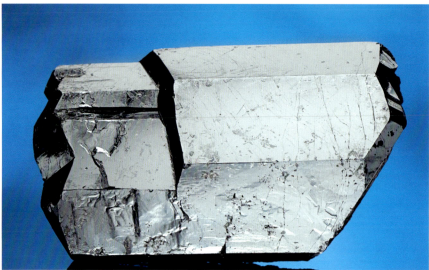

49066   VERY LARGE RUTILE CRYSTAL

Graves Mountain Mines, Graves Mountain, Lincoln Co., Georgia, USA

Over the years, an industrial minerals quarry in Graves Mountain, Georgia, has intermittently produced the largest crystals of Rutile (TiO2) on the planet. Most of these measure no more than 3 to 3½ inches in the longest dimension. At almost seven inches in height, the monster crystal on view here stands far above that. As if that wasn't enough, since it grew resting on its back side, both ends of the crystal were free to develop equally. This is a fairly rare occurrence and it leads to the crystal being "doubly terminated," a condition that adds to the collector value. The crystal is also twinned as evidenced by the "zig-zag" arrangement of terminal faces – not an unusual situation with regards to this material. Rutile has a higher refractive index and dispersion than Diamond which is why synthetic Rutile enjoyed a brief stint as a Diamond simulant in jewelry some years ago. It also accounts for the almost metallic luster displayed by the crystal under virtually all lighting conditions. When you do get past the semi-metallic luster, the Rutile exhibits the deep red coloration that is typical for this material and the locality. At 6½ x 4 x 2¾ inches, it is an enormous Rutile crystal. From the Howard Belsky Collection, it dates to the 1900-1920's. In fact, the Belsky Family donated a smaller specimen to the Smithsonian where it is still on exhibit today. In excellent condition, it has a custom base.

Provenance: Howard Belsky Collection

Estimate: $32,000-$36,000

49067   QUARTZ WITH INCLUSIONS OF PAPAGOITE, KAOLINITE, EPIDOTE & CHLORITE
Messina Mine, Messina District, Limpopo Province, South Africa

Quartz has the endearing quality of often including other minerals that happen to grow on its crystal faces, while the Quartz is still in its growth phase. For reasons known only to Mother Nature, the Quartz Growth Express stopped long enough for delicate blue needles of the rare Copper mineral Papagoite to climb aboard, it then continued onward to further growth. The best extant examples of this combination were mined in 1985 and production has declined since then. Most of the crystals recovered required polishing of faces to remove an opaque coating that obscures the Papagoite from view. This example is one of the rare few that did not require such treatment. Its crystal faces are completely natural. The termination shows regrowth after minor damage sustained while still growing. In addition to the Papagoite, there are clouds of golden hued Kaolinite and an occasional green microcrystal of Epidote and/or "Chlorite." At various times the specimen was owned by Paul Botha, a South African mineral dealer, and was then acquired by collector J.R. Glover in 1997. As is typical for these Quartz specimens, it is without matrix, but it does come with a custom base to orient it properly. Overall measurements are 2⅝ x 1½ x 2 inches and is in excellent condition.
Estimate: $3,250-$3,750

49068   ARKANSAS DIAMOND COLLECTION
Murfreesboro, Pike Co., Arkansas, USA

This collection consists of 35 diamonds ranging from pinhead size to 1.63 carats in weight. All of these diamond crystals are from the Crater of Diamonds near Murfreesboro, Arkansas, and were collected by the Norm Dawson family in the 1950's. The collection contains an assortment of colors, sizes and crystal habits: there is a Macle twin weighing 1.14 cts and at least one perfect octahedron; colors range from colorless to several that look to be "Fancy" in coloration. Norm Dawson was a prominent San Diego County miner who traveled to Arkansas when the Crater of Diamonds was still privately owned. This selection was collected in the 1950's over the course of multiple family vacations and a letter of authentication accompanies the lot. The Crater of Diamonds became a State Park in the 1970's and few documented Diamond crystals survive from earlier times. This many Diamonds from the locality, if found in one year, indeed would be a quite news item.
Estimate: $4,500-$5,500

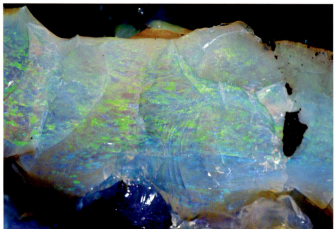 

49069   DRAMATIC BOULDER OPAL
Western Queensland, Australia

Opal miners in Australia work long hot months digging and breaking rock underground in the barren outback looking for opals. Rarely do they find bits of gem opal bigger than a thumbnail, hidden within rust-colored boulders of mudstone. Imagine their amazement and excitement when they broke open a large round boulder and found a dramatic, beautiful, and completely unexpected sea of opal inside. What they found was a massive specimen of boulder opal, which comprise only 2% of all opal found. As masses of mud dry up, internal cracks form, which can fill with silica-infused water that condenses into opal; in this case, a very large series of cracks combined to form a pillared cavity. The cavity filled with silica-rich water during wet seasons to form many layers of rainbow fire opal between the pillars, but the water never lasted long enough to fill the cavity completely with opal. The result is a sea of precious opal with pillars of mudstone rising out of it; the columns are coated with thin veneers of opal from when water did temporarily fill up the entire cavity. The quality of the opal alone makes this a worthwhile specimen; the precious opal has rainbows of color ranging from washes of deep blue to gorgeous turquoise to rich purples along with pinpoints of red and green fire. The swirling browns of the ironstone matrix provide the perfect contrast to offset the dazzling opal. This extraordinary find has never been touched up by man; it demonstrates the dramatic beauty of nature and measures approximately 11 x 6 x 7 inches, presented on a custom metal display stand.
Estimate: $16,000-$20,000

PYRITE

Ampliación a Victoria Mine, Navajún, La Rioja, Spain

49070   EXTREMELY LARGE PYRITE ON MATRIX

"Is that real?" is an often heard comment when a Pyrite specimen from Navajun, Spain, is displayed. People find it hard to believe that this kind of geometric perfection could form without the assistance of humans. These stark cubic forms seem to be machined from solid brass, then highly polished. Normally they are seen *sans* matrix, but occasionally the miner will come up with a matrix specimen for the customers that demand a little more. This example comes from the mine owner's private collection, which is quite understandable when considering that it is composed of 5 perfect cubes ranging in size from 1⅛ to over 4 inches on edge. Anything over 3 inches is large for this locality. In addition, the largest cube features an interpenetrating cube 2¾ inches on edge. The matrix is the typical grey to off-white material normal for such things. Many tons of rock were painstakingly winnowed to produce a specimen this fine. It measures a large 13 x 11 x 9½ inches and is in pristine condition.
Estimate: $42,500-$50,000

PYRITE

Quiruvilca Mine, Quiruvilca District, Santiago de Chuco Province, La Libertad Department, Peru

49071   MUSEUM QUALITY PYRITE

The widespread and common occurrence of Pyrite serves to obscure the fact that large and perfect groups of Pyrite crystals are not common. In the 1970-1980's, the Quiruvilca Mine was a prominent producer of fine Pyrite specimens. It was the source for this exquisitely beautiful group of giant, octahedral crystals – there are no less than 18 separate octahedrons making up this "Mountain of Fool's Gold". Triangular faces, up to 3 inches on edge, display an almost infinite number of negative crystal faces, giving the specimen a brilliantly scintillating appearance. In addition to the size and perfection of the specimen, it was part of the Smithsonian Institution National Museum Collection and it comes with the original Smithsonian label #147880. Accompanied by a custom base, it measures 4¾ inches high by 6½ x 6½ inches.
Provenance: Smithsonian Institution Collection
Estimate: $14,000-$17,000

49072   PYRITE

Huanzala Mine, Huallanca District, Dos de Mayo
Province, Huánuco Department, Peru

Large, freestanding Pyrite crystal groups comprise a very small percentage of those mined every year. As a member of that diminutive fraternity, this aesthetically composed group of crystals flaunts its charm with truly brassy style. The main octahedron is more than respectable at 2⅛ inches across and it is proudly situated upon a group of smaller, though no less perfect, crystals. All of the Pyrite crystals display complex modifications at their vertices, along with stunning brilliance of luster, giving ample reason to study this metallic wonder at close hand. Specimens of this size and perfection of form are very desirable today. In pristine condition with a custom acrylic base, it measures 3¼ x 1⅝ x 2¼ inches.
Provenance: Martin Lewadny Collection of Winnipeg, Canada.
Estimate: $5,750-$6,500

49073   NATIVE COPPER

Keweenaw Peninsula, Michigan

Copper is a metal on the periodic table of elements and has been mined for thousands of years in the Keweenaw Peninsula of Michigan from both Precambrian rocks and glacial deposits. This specimen features a twisted sheet metal appearance that is a classic characteristic of copper specimens found in this region. Bearing white chips of its original calcite matrix and possessing a warm metallic luster, this natural copper specimen makes a bold impression and measures 7½ x 3½ inches.
Estimate: $250-$350

GOLD CRYSTALS

Eagle's Nest Mine (Mystery Wind Mine), Placer Co., California, USA

49074 NATIVE GOLD CRYSTALS ON MATRIX

Crystalline Gold specimens have always represented a very small percentage of the World supply of this, much sought after, fought over, metal. Based upon collector preferences, certain criteria define the ideal Gold specimen. Some of the more important ones are: a) The presence of large, well-defined, undamaged crystals; b) Specula rather than matte luster; c) High percentage of actual Gold for richness of color; d) Presence of host rock matrix; e) Aesthetic arrangement of crystals; f) Freedom from "enhancements" or exotic treatments, i.e. acid etching of host rock; and finally g) Overall size of specimen. With due consideration to the above criteria, close inspection of this reticulated mass of Native Gold leads to a fairly obvious conclusion: this is an exceptional specimen of the metal that any museum would be proud to display side by side with equally exceptional historic jewels. The form seems to grow as it rises from a white Quartz matrix, with splashes of burnt sienna surrounding spots of included Gold. The luster and color are as good as it gets for this metal, showing rich, buttery reflections from a multitude of shining faces. There is no damage to mar the beauty of this carefully conserved wonder. The overall dimensions of the piece are 7½ inches high by 2 inches wide by 1 inch thick. A stunning addition to any serious collection. It has a custom labeled acrylic base.
Provenance: Lyda Hill Collection, Dallas, Texas
Estimate: $170,000-$225,000

GOLD NUGGET

Kingower Gold Field, Western Australia

49075   MASSIVE GOLD NUGGET

Gold nuggets over five ounces are extremely rare, with fewer than five generally being discovered worldwide each year. The Kingower Gold Field of Western Australia, however, is famed for producing more than its fair share, having yielded the largest nugget ever found with a metal detector, the 61 lb "Hand of Faith" discovered in 1980. The present specimen falls short of that size but is still a monster, with a fantastically convoluted form: some surfaces of this natural nugget resemble solidified liquid streams while other areas have the appearance of crumpled gold leaf. Twisted and folded with apertures, concavities and crevices throughout, the protruding sections are rubbed to a burnished smoothness and visible throughout are the remains of the quartz-rich host rock in which the gold originally crystallized. A superb, large and aesthetic example it measures approximately 5⅛ x 4⅛ x 2½ inches and weighs 59.41 troy oz (1848g).
Estimate: $125,000-$140,000

49076   LARGE GOLD NUGGET

Victoria, Australia

A hefty specimen for the collector with a weakness for precious metals in serious chunks, this 700 gram nugget from Victoria, Australia, is large enough to be dangerous if dropped or thrown for that matter, at or on someone. Aside from its potential as a blunt instrument, it represents a solid investment in these times of shaky equity. That the nugget is high Karat is evidenced by the rich ... well ... "GOLDEN" color it displays, not the pallid yellow of 10K jewelry. There are a number of included white quartz pebbles that show no signs of etching or other treatments. Besides its significance based on size and purity, it has the added cachet of having been owned by Dr. Ed David, Science & Technology Advisor to President Nixon. It bears his accession number "107P". In size, it spans 3 inches wide by 1¾ inches high by 1 inch thick and weighs 22.51 troy oz (700.1g). There is a custom, labeled base.

Estimate: $35,000-$40,000

49077   GOLD NUGGET

Laverton, Western Australia

This elongated nugget has been rubbed almost completely smooth on its raised surfaces, suggesting a long water-tumbled journey from the ancient mountains to the desolate outback. In pleasing contrast, however, it retains some excellent texture to the deeper crevices of its folded form, as well as fragments of the original quartz-rich rock in which it crystallized. The strong bright yellow color denotes a high karat content and the smooth surfaces give it a brilliant luster. An excellent specimen, it measures approximately 2⅞ x 1⅜ x ¾ inches and weighs in at 6.20 troy oz (193g).

Estimate: $12,000-$14,000

49078 NATIVE GOLD NUGGET
Kalgoorlie, Western Australia

This spiky little nugget has a fantastically twisted three-dimensionality to it and an incredible texture; only very small portions of the protruding areas have been rubbed smooth by erosion and the rest of the pitted pocketed surface is textured with jagged peaks and ridges. Australian gold is notable for its purity and the bright yellow color of the present example bears out that reputation. A fine aesthetic specimen it measures approximately 2¼ x 1⅝ x 1½ inches and weighs 3.71 troy oz (115.4g).

Estimate: $6,500-$7,000

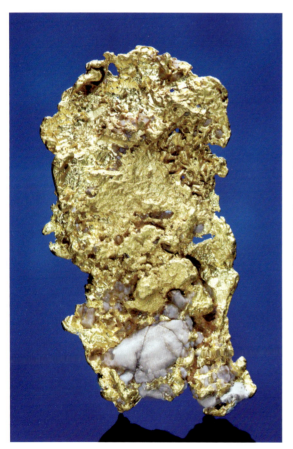

49079 NATIVE GOLD WITH QUARTZ
Victoria, Australia

Gold has a special place as a motivator for a large part of human behavior, and one look at the rich and unique, buttery color – along with the impressive weight of this metal is quite enough to supply the "why." No other material has held this level of fascination, or in some cases: obsession, for Mankind. Virtually as found, this semi-crystallized mass of high karat Gold retains a number of Quartz pebbles that were incorporated at the time of its formation. The condition of the Quartz argues that the specimen has not been etched out of any surrounding rock but rather, simply cleaned of dirt and adhering detritus. It measures 2⅝ x 1½ x ⅜ inches, producing the visual effect of a lot of Gold for only a small amount of it: a good display value. It weighs 2.278 troy oz (70.87g) and comes on a custom base.

Estimate: $5,750-$6,500

49080   LARGE NATIVE SILVER SPECIMEN

Pöhla-Tellerhäuser Mine, Pöhla, Schwarzenberg District, Erzgebirge, Saxony, Germany

Among Silver's various forms, or "habits" as mineralogists call them, is the arborescent type that resembles conifer branches. This extreme example is characterised by delicate crystal growths that look like metallic "feathers" frozen in the host rock. The dark matrix rock formed contemporaneously with, or shortly after, the Silver; incorporating and protecting the "feathers" from mechanical damage. At some stage, the surface matrix was slightly dissolved revealing these delicate shining forms to the miner and ultimately to the World. This unusual type of Native Silver is instantly recognizable as being from Pöhla in Saxony, Germany, source of a number of finely crystallized exotic minerals.

This cabinet specimen has individual "feathers" extending to approximately 1 inch in length and there are numerous ones generously distributed all over. There is a small "porthole" extending from one side of the specimen to the other, allowing a glimpse into the interior where more "feathers" are eternally trapped in their dark prison. There are traces of another, white mineral, possibly Quartz, and it has a custom acrylic base. Quite sizable at 6½ x 6½ x 2½ inches, it is in excellent condition and is from an old East Coast collection.

Estimate: $15,000-$18,000

49081   PLATINUM NUGGET WITH CRYSTALLINE FACES

Citoco District, Chocó Department, Colombia

Rarer by far than Gold, Platinum has exerted a subtle but undeniable force in the pantheon of valuable things that people and empires have fought over. As commonly encountered, most Platinum is in the form of an occasional microscopic grain intermixed with large quantities of worthless rock. Very rarely, nuggets and crystals of this precious metal appear in the "concentrate" of placer mines or even more rarely, in a placer miner's gold pan. It was this situation that brought the "large old time nugget with crystalline surfaces" to light many years ago, as referenced in the accompanying label. Until 1820, Colombia was the only known source for Platina or "the little Silver" and, even in Colombia, it was considered a nuisance because everyone was searching for and extracting Gold and Silver, not this worthless rubbish.

This rather sizable "nugget" shows traces of another associated, dark, granular mineral, presumably an ultramafic one that normally accompanies Platinum. There is a a flat surface on one side giving credence to the idea that at one time the nugget was somewhat larger. Very minor surface rounding shows that the nugget had not traveled far, or for long, from its origin. Originally a gift from noted New York gem and mineral dealer, Allan Caplan, to the American Museum of Natural History. It was subsequently traded/sold to longtime New York mineral dealer Lawrence Conklin and bears his personal collection number 276. This exotic specimen, with its very interesting pedigree, is for serious collectors interested in history as well as worth. It is approximately ¾ of an inch in the longest direction.

Provenance: American Museum of Natural History; Lawrence Conklin Collection

Estimate: $2,800-$3,200

49082   FINE AMETHYST GEODE PAIR
Brazil

This excellent sliced geode boasts lovely gemmy deep purple crystals with excellent consistency of coloring. The sliced faces have been polished and exhibit minimal agate banding; instead, the purple of the crystals shades to white quartz, framed with an orange-brown band of the Madeira citrine color. Each has a gently curving form and one boasts a dramatic little growth of chalky calcite. A fine pair, they measure 43½ and 44 inches high.
Estimate: $3,500-$4,500

49083   CITRINE GEODE PAIR
Rio Grande do Sul, South Region, Brazil

Citrine is one of the most desirable forms of quartz, valued in ancient times when it was thought to offer protection from snake venom and "evil thoughts". It is also known as the "success stone" or "merchant's stone" and said to attract wealth and prosperity if carried on the person or positioned correctly in the home or place of business. This beautiful pair of geodes, or "cathedrals", boasts lovely crystals of the finest deep Madeira color, studded with a few growths of large chalky quartz crystals and strikingly framed by the white quartz of the cut and polished face, in a slender, curving pair of chimneys 50⅜ and 49¼ inches tall.
Estimate: $4,000-$5,000

49084   LAPIS LAZULI FREEFORM
Badakhshan, Afghanistan
Of the highest quality Lapis lazuli, this beautiful freeform has been finished with a highly lustrous polish to show off the fantastic color and patterning of the semi-precious gem material. On a gorgeous rich blue ground, speckles of silvery pyrite and faint white calcite veins swirl like some distant galaxy, and the piece has been artfully oriented such that two opposing faces feature vertical streams of the inclusions: as the poet said, "Every discoloration of the stone / Every accidental crack or dent / Seems a water course or an avalanche / Or lofty slope where it still snows" (no cracks present here). A gorgeous decorative object, it measures 14⅜ x 7 x 5⅜ inches.
Estimate: $3,000-$4,000

49085   LAPIS LAZULI FREEFORM
Badakhshan, Afghanistan
Lapis lazuli has been mined in Afghanistan for over 6000 years, highly prized for its gorgeous deep blue color, and lapis jewelry has been found pre-dynastic Egyptian sites and as far from Afghanistan as Neolithic sites in Mauritania. The lovely galactic patterning in this rich azure stone is caused by the presence of silvery gold pyrite and faint white calcite veins; this highly polished freeform has been artfully oriented such that two opposite faces feature these inclusions running in parallel streams vertically down the piece. A gorgeous decorative object, it measures 10¼ x 6⅝ x 3¼ inches.
Estimate: $2,400-$3,000

49086   POLISHED LABRADORITE FREEFORM
Madagascar

This is an especially good specimen of labradorite, the highly collectible feldspar mineral that lends its name to the optical phenomenon "labradorescence". A form of schiller effect, this phenomenon occurs when alternating layers of feldspar crystals reflect only those light waves of the proper wavelength, or color, resulting in an incredibly shimmering display that seems to emanate from just beneath the surface of the rock itself. Not all labradorite specimens exhibit this characteristic, but it is present all over this highly polished freeform, and one face flashes with bands of gold, green and electric blue across the entirety of its flat surface. In addition to its excellent labradorescence, this is a good-sized specimen, and measures 11½ x 7½ x 3½ inches. There is one small chip at the top of the matrix, otherwise in fine condition.
Estimate: $900-$1,200

49087   DOUBLE HEART RAINBOW OBSIDIAN SCULPTURE
Mexico

Rainbow obsidian is volcanic silica glass, differing from regular obsidian in that the lamellar crystallites orientate parallel to the flow structure to produce an ethereal colored banding. This is beautiful enough in itself, but here the master lapidarist has carved a single piece in such a way that the bands of color form a pair of hearts of perfect concentric form in lovely soft shades of purple, yellow and green. Also known as "fire" or "iris" obsidian, it is regarded in crystallographic metaphysics to act as a particularly powerful aid to meditation, helping the user to combat shock, fear or barriers, but a piece such as this is also an elegant and skillfully executed sculpture, brought to a gleaming polished finish and measuring 9½ x 3¼ x 3¼ inches.
Estimate: $800-$1,000

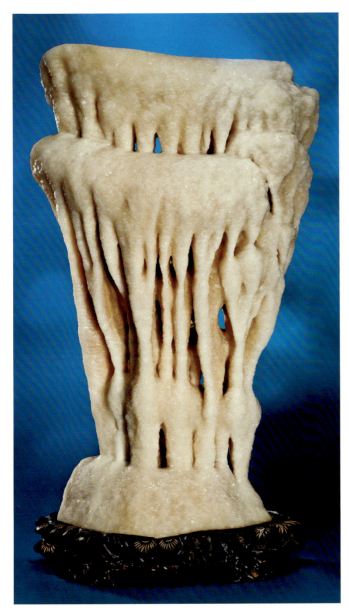

49088 "WATERFALL" STALACTITE
China

This wonderful natural sculpture is from the deep caves of the Hubai Province in east-central China. The caves have been flooded to create the Three Gorges Dam reservoir, and luckily, just prior to the flooding, some ambitious miners were able to gain access and remove several portions of the cave walls along with some stalactite formations so that these natural wonders would be saved from destruction. This stalactite formed over many many years, as calcite-bearing waters dripped from the cave's ceiling almost imperceptibly deposited their load to build up this fantastic concretion. With an uncanny symmetry, it looks like a cluster of sparkling icicles. Presented on a carved wooden base and measures 37¼ inches high.

Estimate: $1,400-$1,800

49089 LARGE STALACTITE
China

Glistening as though still wet with the mineral-rich water from which it formed over countless painstaking years, this fascinating natural sculpture is from the ancient caves of central China, now submerged deep beneath the massive Three Gorges Reservoir. Its undulating form and smooth surface are evocative of the slow process of deposition and the calcite impurities from which it formed have imparted to it a two-tone coloring, half pale gray-cream and half a warm soft orange tan. Nature at its most sculptural, it stands 59 inches high on a carved wooden base.

Estimate: $1,800-$2,400

49090   TIGER IRON SLAB

Paleoproterozoic
Port Hedland, Western Australia
This beautiful slab of tiger iron is an excellent example of the distinctive banding formed in the stone by folded layers of flashing golden tiger's eye, red jasper, hematite (iron oxide) and stromatolite. This last constituent represents the oldest organism in the fossil record, the 2½ billion year old remains of cyanobacteria or algae; in converting carbon dioxide, water and sunlight into our planet's first oxygen atmosphere, these primitive life forms played a fundamental role in creating the world as we know it. Here they are preserved in beautifully decorative form, as part of this fine irregularly-shaped slab 39⅝ x 20 x ½ inches.
Estimate: $3,500-$4,500

49091   FINE MARRA MAMBA TIGER-EYE SLAB

Maramamba, south-western Australia
Collected and treasured for thousands of years as an ornamental jewelry stone, tiger eye is found today mainly in African and Australian copper belts. One of the very rarest varieties, however, is this multi-colored Marra Mamba material, found only in the blue crocidolite (asbestos) seams of the Hamersley Range in the Pilbara region of Western Australia. This incredible example of nature's abstract artistry is comprised of shimmering hematite, chatoyant tiger's eye and fossilized algae-derived stromatolite, layered in between colorful jasper in generous bands that seem to drip and flow into one another. A large and beautiful example, the slab is backed with a metal support and measures 38¾ x 16⅛ x ⅜ inches.
Estimate: $6,500-$7,500

49092 AN EXCEPTIONAL GEM KUNZITE

Spodumene (variety kunzite)
Brazil

Most gemstones are already rare in some way: otherwise they would not be as valued as they are. The truly exceptional must prove their rarity in many ways and – given the inherent scarcity of the raw material, its top-notch gemological qualities, pedigreed provenance and documentation – such is the case with this remarkable faceted kunzite.

Among the mineral species that make up the Earth's crust, spodumene is not at all abundant, yet in very few places in the earth, it occurs in small deposits rich enough to be considered an ore of lithium and as crystals to some 6 meters long. Many orders of magnitude less common are gem quality crystals of the mineral. Since being first described in 1800, spodumene remained off the aesthetic radar for 80 years until the discovery of its green gem variety, hiddenite, which became, and still is, highly prized. A little more than 20 years later, a find of limpid lilac crystals in California – varietally named kunzite, after noted Tiffany gemologist, G.F. Kunz – changed the status of spodumene to that of a bona fide gem species. The reality remains that gem quality kunzite represents only the tiniest fraction of the spodumene known.

At over 722 carats and measuring approximately 42.95 x 39.25 x 43.85 mm, this modified rectangular (emerald) step cut gem is among the giants for kunzite. It is the largest of four significantly large stones that were cut in 1981 by John Ramsey and Tom Carleton from a one-kilogram crystal that, 25 years prior to Ramsey's acquisition of it, had been taken across the Atlantic from Brazil to reside in a European collection. Only in Brazil have gem crystals large enough to produce this size and quality been unearthed. Ramsey's comments regarding the rough crystal:

"It should first be mentioned that the availability of a one-kilo, essentially clean kunzite crystal from Brazil in today's marketplace is in itself a phenomenon. Certainly, a number of fine crystals from Brazil were available in the late 1950's and early 1960's, but these disappeared from the market some time ago. Afghanistan produces kunzite, but nothing of the size and quality of the crystal described."[1]

This superbly cut stone is in the same elite size league as the Smithsonian Institution's 880 carat kunzite. However, in a letter, renowned gemological authority, Joel Arem, wrote in comparison that "the 722 [carats] from this crystal [are] far superior in color and cut with both deep saturation and high brilliancy." He also declared that "I believe that nobody would argue against the premise that the number of stones against which this [stone] might be compared can be counted on one hand."[2] Arem underscored this belief when he chose a photograph of this specimen to illustrate the gem species in his popular *Color Encyclopedia of Gemstones.*[3]

Ramsey described in detail the process and difficulties of cutting kunzite in general, and this stone in particular, in a 1981 article published in the internationally leading gemological journal, *Gems & Gemology.* Kunzite is trichroic, meaning it exhibits different colors in 3 directions, and one of the important decisions the cutters made was to produce several stones out of the one kilo rough crystal rather than one single gem. In doing so, they maximized the color intensity. Any other direction would have produced either a much paler purple or even a near colorless to pale green...one can imagine since the trichroism is still wonderfully apparent when viewed in the appropriate directions. This sort of documentation, in addition to the gemstone encyclopedia entry and a Gemological Institute of America (GIA) certificate[4] confirming the gem material identity, adds significant collector appeal and value over and above the stone's superlative inherent qualities.

Rare gem material, superb craftsmanship, stature and a documented history make this museum-quality gem a true rarity.

[1] Ramsey, J. "The Cutting Properties of Kunzite" *Gems & Gemology*, winter 1981. Detailed account of the cutting of the rough from which this stone came.
[2] Arem, J. Letter dated 2/26/93. States "world's finest cut kunzite".
[3] Arem, J. *Color Encyclopedia of Gemstones*, Second Edition, 1987. Index section of color photographs, #215.
[4] Gemological Institute of America Identification Report 4254632, dated 12/01/93.

Estimate: $27,500-$35,000

49093   KUNZITE
Afghanistan

Named for George Kunz, chief gemologist and consultant to Tiffany et Cie, Kunzite is the lilac to pink variety of gem Spodumene. Never particularly common, Kunzite remains a gemstone found chiefly in sophisticated and museum collections. This cushion cut example shows a lovely pink body color with peach highlights. At 48.50 carats it is a large gemstone best suited for a pendant or brooch, although a ring is not out of the question. It measures 23.5 x 20.5 mm.

Estimate: $2,000-$2,500

49094   EXCEPTIONALLY LARGE CALIFORNIA TOURMALINE
Tourmaline Queen Mine, California

One of the best sources of exceptional tourmalines in the world happens to be in California; the Pala mining district located outside of San Diego has produced a few rare but exceptionally beautiful tourmalines that grace the collections of museums around the world. The mining claims in Pala were first worked in the early 1900's but abandoned in 1911 because the cost of mining outweighed the profits from the gems. Mining picked up in the late 1960's and tourmaline crystals of exceptional color and quality were found in hidden vugs throughout the mining district. This gemstone originated from the Tourmaline Queen Mine and was meticulously cut by German artists from Idar-Oberstein in the 1980's; the resulting piece is an extraordinary large and clear pink tourmaline gem. The clarity of this gem is distinguished and although the cut is not perfect; it's still quite good for its impressive size of 82.83 carats.

Estimate: $18,000-$22,000

49095   RARE GEMSTONE: PINK FLUORITE
Pakistan

Due to the rarity of suitable rough, the pink color variant of Fluorite is not often seen in gem collections. With the recent availability of large, somewhat "bruised" Fluorite crystals from Pakistan, there is now an occasional cut stone appearing on the market. This light pink trillion style stone was cut from just such material. There are a few minor inclusions, but they are confined to areas near the girdle and require specialized lighting to be visible. The stone is otherwise clean, bright and cut at the proper angles for Fluorite. It measures 27.4 x 24.2 x 23.4 mm and weighs 48.01 cts.

Estimate: $1,500-$2,000

49096   RARE GEMSTONE: COLOR CHANGE FLUORITE
Morocco

A number of gemstones have the exotic property of "color change," a formal term in gemology that indicates a shift in apparent color of a given gemstone induced by changes in the color temperature of the light used to view the stone. In practical terms this is usually defined by changes in a gemstones appearance under: artificial light (fluorescent, incandescent, candlelight, etc.) versus natural daylight. The intensity of the effect can range from very subtle to quite obvious. In the case of this oval brilliant cut Fluorite, the color change goes from a pale lavender tint under incandescent or candlelight, to a powder blue under daylight or similar color temperature illumination. There is an incipient cleavage near the girdle but otherwise the stone is eye-clean, bright and well proportioned. This rare gemstone measures 24.6 x 18.6 mm and weighs 42.16 cts.

Estimate: $1,400-$1,800

49097   RARE GEMSTONE: GREEN FLUORITE
Afghanistan

In addition to being a source for flying lead, Afghanistan in its more peaceful moments, has produced some very notable examples of green Fluorite that are large and transparent enough to furnish significant cut gemstones for the sophisticated collectors of the world. This rectangular oval cushion style stone displays a mint green body color that is very similar to a light Tsavorite green. The stone is well cut and polished, and is quite clean with the minor exception of a few minute, pinpoint inclusions visible under high-power lighting. This rare collector gemstone measures 24.9 x 15.5 mm and weighs 35.59 cts.

Estimate: $1,200-$1,500

49098   RARE GEMSTONE: HIDDENITE
Brazil

Originally, the term "Hiddenite" referred strictly to the green variety of Spodumene from Hiddenite, North Carolina. Over time all green Spodumene gems have come to be called Hiddenite. In the case of the oval brilliant cut stone seen here, the origin was the Minas Gerais area of Brazil. The stone displays a pale green body color that accentuates the high levels of both transparency and scintillation. There is a tiny inclusion above the culet, otherwise this rather large stone is quite clean. It measures 25.0 x 19.0 mm and weighs a considerable 41.55 cts.

Estimate: $1,600-$2,000

49099   RARE GEMSTONE: RAINBOW CALCITE
Brazil

Calcite is easily one of the most commonly encountered minerals on the planet. In spite of this fact, the amount of transparent and colorless Calcite that has been mined is minuscule by comparison. The largest proportion of this paltry production has gone for components in expensive optical gear. A small percentage of this material is "twinned," the result of two crystals growing through each other. Twinned Calcite has the striking property of producing rainbow colored reflections from certain planes within the material. This mixed cut stone shows phenomenal flashes of spectral fire off of those planes when oriented properly. It measures 25.9 x 16.6 mm and weighs in at 37.33 cts.

Estimate: $1,200-$1,600

49100   RARE GEMSTONE: SPHALERITE
Spain

Sphalerite (ZnS) is the principal ore of Zinc. Although widely distributed around the globe, it is not usually found in transparent crystals light enough in color and with sufficient clarity, to furnish facetted gems. The mines of Picos de Europa in the Pyrenees of Spain are one of the exceptions to this rule. Here orange-red globular crystal groups attain sizes of 2 to 4 inches in diameter. Clear areas within these aggregates are occasionally saved for cutting by master gem cutters skilled enough to handle this difficult material. This golden round brilliant gemstone shows the exceptionally brilliant adamantine luster and extreme dispersion that Sphalerite is known for. There are several tiny, unobtrusive inclusions near the the girdle, otherwise the stone is quite clean. It measures 14.4 mm in diameter and weighs 15.24 cts.

Estimate: $750-$1,000

49101 RARE GEMSTONE: SCAPOLITE
Tanzania

Scapolite is a gem material, rarely seen outside of museum collections; it is a complex mineral that rarely forms crystals transparent enough to be facetted. The material from Morogoro, Tanzania, typically presents itself in the honey-gold coloration displayed by the oval brilliant stone seen here. It can very easily be mistaken for Citrine, however, any number of physical properties such as the deep red fluorescence displayed by this stone can be used to differentiate from the more common gem materials that resemble it. There are a few "feather" type inclusions present but they require considerable diligence to be observed. This rare gemstone measures 24.7 x 17.9 mm and weighs 30.06 cts.
Estimate: $1,400-$1,800

49102 YELLOW SPODUMENE
Brazil

Unlike lilac Kunzite or green Hiddenite, the yellow variety of Spodumene has yet to acquire a varietal name. As a result, it is stuck with a simply descriptive name: Yellow Spodumene – not the best way to achieve "brand name recognition." That, coupled with its relative rarity, condemn it to appearances in the cabinets of rare stone collectors and museums. Cut in a round brilliant style, this rather sizable gem is bright and lively with a pleasing Chardonnay tint. It measures 21.1 mm in diameter and it weighs 35.40 cts.
Estimate: $800-$1,100

49103 TANZANITE
Merelani Hills, Lelatema Mts, Arusha Region, Tanzania

Discovered relatively recently, in 1967, the blue-purple variety of Zoisite referred to as "Tanzanite" is one of the hotter items on the gem market today. The best stones such as this trillion style gemstone displays a deep blue violet coloration with occasional flashes of reddish purple. Increasing costs in mining and decreasing production have had the effect of driving prices higher over time, making Tanzanite one of the better bets in gem investing these days. This eye-clean trillion measures 14.4 x 14.3 x 13.9 mm and weighs 13.07 cts.
Estimate: $9,000-$13,000

49104 BRIGHT GREEN PERIDOT
Pakistan

With the discovery of significant Peridot resources in Pakistan, the world has seen the arrival of cut stones whose size, color and clarity would have been strictly imaginary in times before. This light green trillion style stone is enormous when considered against extant examples from Arizona, Egyptian and Burmese sources. It is even large by Pakistan standards. There are a few minor inclusions that are only noticeable under high-power lighting conditions, otherwise it is clean and bright. It measures 19.5 x 18.8 x 19.3 mm and weighs 18.42 cts.
Estimate: $3,250-$3,750

49105 ANDRADITE GARNET
Mexico

Two of the reasons for the popularity of Diamond as a gemstone are the extremely high Refractive Index (R.I.) and a very high Dispersion. Andradite, one of the many varieties of Garnet, also has extremely high values for these properties. As a result the round brilliant cut Andradite seen here possesses excellent "fire" which is particularly apparent when the stone is being moved about. The golden-brown body color is light enough that the strong dispersion shows very well. Fashioned from Mexican material the stone is quite clean and well cut and measures 8.9 mm in diameter and weighs 3.07 cts.
Estimate: $1,800-$2,200

49106   SUITE OF BERYL GEMSTONES
1. Aqua, Nigeria; 2. Heliodor, Brazil; 3. Chrome Beryl, Nigeria; 4. Morganite, Mozambique

This four gem suite is eminently suitable for inclusion in a comparative collection of the various types and localities of Beryl. It features examples of several of the major color varieties of this mineral: Aquamarine, Heliodor, Chrome Beryl and Morganite. The Aquamarine from Nigeria is cut in a trillion style and shows good depth of color in a stone of this size. Clean and well proportioned, it measures 9.3 x 9.5 x 9.2 mm and weighs 2.30 cts. The second gemstone of the suite is a golden Heliodor from Brazil. It was cut in a square scissors style and is eye clean. The measurements of this golden jewel are 12.0 x 10.1 mm and the weight is 5.08 cts. The third in the series is an eye clean Chrome Beryl from Nigeria. This material is quite rare for Beryl. High levels of Chromium in Beryl are responsible for the gem we call Emerald. In this instance the lower Chromium levels and appearance are such that the material doesn't quite qualify as Emerald but with some Vanadium and low Iron it can't be considered Aquamarine either, hence the default use of chemical nomenclature in the name. This attractive blue-green emerald cut gemstone measures 9.1 x 7.1 mm and weighs 2.21 cts. The fourth member of the suite is a Morganite, the pink color variety in Beryl. It was mined in the former Portuguese colony of Mozambique. The cut style is a simple, oval brilliant with excellent proportions and scintillation. It measures 11.5 x 8.2 mm and weighs 2.74 cts.

Estimate: $1,400-$1,800

49107   SUITE OF GEMSTONES: QUARTZ WITH INCLUSIONS
Brazil

This group of three Brazilian Quartz gemstones have a unique feature in common: they all have exceptional examples of other minerals as inclusions. The first is a rectangular emerald cut colorless Quartz with a euhedral Pyrite crystal directly under the table of the stone. It measures 18.2 x 13.8 mm and weighs 17.89 cts. The second is also clear Quartz that features a golden hued crystal of Calcite centered under the table of a "stretched" hexagon style of cut. It is 19.2 x 14.5 mm and weighs 14.19 cts. The third gemstone in this suite is a colorless, slightly "sleepy" emerald cut stone with a brassy Marcasite "bloom" floating just above the culet. This final gemstone measures 13.6 x 12.6 mm and weighs 9.97 cts.

Estimate: $1,200-$1,600

49108   MONTANA SAPPHIRE: ROUGH & CUT SET
Yogo Gulch, Yogo District, Little Belt Mts, Judith Basin Co., Montana, USA

Few people outside of the gem trade are aware of the fine quality Sapphires that have been mined in the Yogo Gulch area of Montana. Given that the production over the years has been small, it is a testament to the quality of the gem material that mining is still viable in this uniquely American mine. The matched "rough & cut" set seen here features a beautiful, facetted example of classic "cornflower" blue hue accompanied by an actual piece of the uncut Sapphire from this little-known gem mine. The pear-shaped gemstone is quite clean and it weighs 1.16 cts while measuring 8.15 x 5.88 mm. The crystal fragment weighs in at 2.35 cts and measures 9.8 x 6.84 mm. Both are from the collection of Dan Mayer of Sun City, Idaho, who was a prominent exploration geologist in the 1950's.

Estimate: $3,000-$4,000

49109   PERIDOT: ROUGH & CUT SET
St John's Island, Red Sea, Egypt

St. Johns Island, a small speck of land off the Red Sea coast of Egypt appears as if it was the victim of massive artillery bombardment continuing for decades. Known since antiquity as a source for Peridot, August's birthstone, this blasted landscape has not suffered from war so much as incessant operations designed to pry this lovely green gem from the dark, volcanic clutches of the island's lava flows. Several millenia of dedicated hammering has resulted in very little Peridot being discovered there anymore. This makes a rough and cut set of this historic material a bit of a rarity. The set consists of a well-formed, double Peridot crystal of medium green color weighing 41.7 cts and a facetted round brilliant gemstone, cut from the same material, weighing 3.33 cts. The Peridot "rough" measures 23.78 x 22.78 x 11.8 mm while the cut stone is 9 mm in diameter. The back side of the crystal shows a break and there are some brownish inclusions in fractures. Luster is typical, with fine striations being visible on exposed faces. The gemstone is quite clean with a minuscule carbon spot. The crystal is Ex Gerald Herfurth Collection #2702 and previously was part of the E.M. Gunnell collection # 4-18-53. The cut stone is Ex Herb Obodda.

Estimate: $5,000-$6,000

49110   ROUGH AND CUT AMETRINE CRYSTALS
Anahi Mine, Bolivia

Ametrine is a rare form of quartz that is part amethyst and part citrine. Temperature gradients cause different oxidation states of iron in quartz, resulting in zonings of purple and yellow. Natural ametrine is extremely rare and only occurs in Bolivia and a handful of other countries. This large uncut ametrine crystal specimen features a rich purple amethyst with vertical zones of amber-colored citrine. The emerald-cut gem also displays the zoning between purple and yellow. Both of these are natural specimens that have not been enhanced; the crystal specimens measures 5¼ x 2¾ x 2¼ inches and the cut stone measures 31 x 23 x 13 mm and weighs 82.52 carats.

Estimate: $600-$800

49111   ROUGH AND CUT SET OF PINK TOURMALINE MUSHROOMS
Momeik, Burma

One of the odd crystal forms of tourmaline are the "mushroom" shaped structures that come from Burma. These tourmalines are very rare and it's especially difficult to find one with an attractive pink color such as this present specimen. The crystal specimen comes paired with a cabochon polished from another mushroom tourmaline to show off the even pink color that can be attained from polishing these unique crystals. The uncut crystal specimen weighs 14.4 grams and measures 1⅜ x ¾ x ½ inches. The cabochon weighs 21.35 carats and measures 18 x 16.5 x 10 mm.

Estimate: $550-$750

49112   RARE GEMSTONE: "CAT'S EYE" TOURMALINE
Afghanistan
Tiny parallel "tube" type inclusions are responsible for the chatoyant "eye" displayed by this Tourmaline cabochon. The light green color is enhanced by the medium height of the dome portion of the stone. The "eye" is sharply defined, seeming to float in the almost transparent body of the stone. There are some healed fracture type inclusions but the "eye" tends to obscure them. This rare cabochon measures 13.1 x 11.7 mm and weighs 8.35 cts.
Estimate: $900-$1,100

49113   RARE GEMSTONE: SMITHSONITE
Choix, Mexico
If fine Jade came in a teal blue version it would look like this double-sided cabochon. It could also be easily mistaken for an exceptionally fine piece of gem Chrysocolla as well, but for its weight – it is much heavier than a comparably sized Chrysocolla cabochon. The low dome of the cabochon allows enough light through the stone to highlight its jelly-like translucency. There are some inclusions but the translucent nature of the material renders their presence functionally irrelevant. This rare gemstone measures 22.7 x 15.5 mm and weighs 26.23 cts.
Estimate: $1,800-$2,200

49114   MOONSTONE
Burma
"Moonstone" is a somewhat ill-defined term that has been applied to a whole host of lapidary materials including several types of Agate. Used in the strictest sense, it can only be applied to certain Feldspars possessed of microperthitic twinning. This twinning is directly responsible for the chatoyant, "floating cloud" effect that gemologists refer to as "schiller." The elongate cabochon seen here is quite transparent for this gem material and it has a very minor amount of inclusions; mostly sub-parallel "feathers." The Schiller displayed is of the colorless type making this a "Silver Flash" type of Moonstone. It measures 20.4 x 12.2 mm and weighs 16.52 cts.
Estimate: $1,400-$1,800

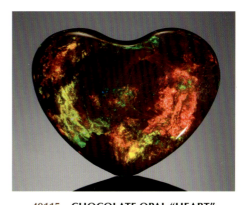

49115   CHOCOLATE OPAL "HEART"
Ethiopia
The last few years have seen Ethiopia joining the ranks of the gem producing nations of the world. The reason for this rise from obscurity has everything to do with the discovery of a new type of fire opal with a unique chocolate body color. The deep, rich brown coloration of this example is shot through with broad flashes of red, green, gold, blue and purple fire. Cut as a fancy heart-shaped cabochon this dark treasure measures 21.5 x 16.1 mm and weighs 10.55 cts.
Estimate: $1,100-$1,400

49116   BLACK OPAL DOUBLET
Australia
Suitable for a brooch or possibly a pendant, this sizable black opal doublet is considerably larger than normal for such things. It exhibits a combination of broad flash and pinfire patterns of fire, predominately of green and gold hues along with occasional flashes of red and deep purple against a dark body color. It is cabochon cut with a low dome and excellent polish. The condition is quite excellent, particularly for an older piece. It measures an impressive 55 x 35 mm (2⅛ x 1⅜ inches).
Provenance: Howard Belsky Collection
Estimate: $750-$1,250

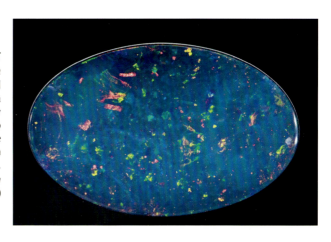

49117   JADE LAMP SHADE
Artist: Barry de Socarras

This beautiful tapering hexagonal lampshade has been fashioned in the stained-glass style of lead caming with thinly sliced and polished "panes" of nephrite jade. Ranging from deep to pale green the individual sections are attractively flecked with black manganese, arranged to create a charming geometric design. Raised on a bronzed tulip-form stand and foliate base it stands 20 inches high, signed, numbered 731 and dated '10.

Estimate: $1,800-$2,400

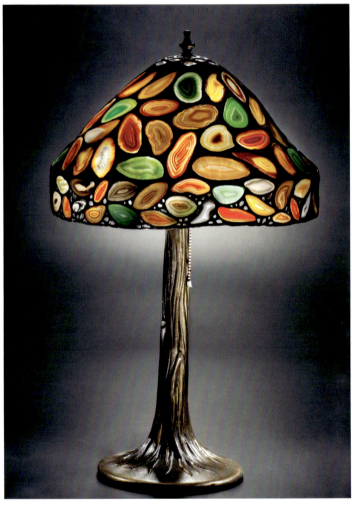

49118   TIFFANY-STYLE AGATE LAMP SHADE
Artist: Barry de Socarras

Using the lead came technique, artist Barry de Socorras creates these beautiful Tiffany-style lamp shades with a variety of natural polished stones. The present example is fashioned from numerous pieces of variously colored translucent agate, creating a beautiful stained glass effect even when unilluminated; when the bulb is turned on, however, it springs into beautiful life, with the lovely warm light taking on hues of green, yellow, orange and red. Raised on a bronzed tree-trunk table stand, it measures 23 inches high, signed, numbered 732 and dated '10.

Estimate: $800-$1,200

49119   TIFFANY-STYLE AMBER LAMP

The domed shade of this lamp has been constructed using the Tiffany-style lead came technique whereby the edges of small translucent components are coated in lead and soldered together to create a stained glass effect. In the present instance, however, it is not glass that has been used, but ancient fossilized tree resin. Each nugget-like section is a piece of Baltic amber, in a wondrous array of orange and yellow shades and the effect when illuminated is a gorgeous and calming golden glow. No wonder that crystal metaphysics considers amber to be a powerful agent for absorbing pain and negativity and for cleansing of the chakra. Raised on a bronze tree-form lamp-stand, the whole beautiful piece measures 16½ inches high.

Estimate: $2,200-$2,600

49120   MATCHED PAIR OF ONYX LAMPS

Handcrafted in Mexico

This unusual pair of decorative accent lamps was painstakingly fashioned from banded Calcite (Travertine Onyx) so that the patterning on one, mirrors the patterning on the other – and the top is matched with each of the four sides. Strongly colored areas of rich red and deep golden brown, contrast strongly with zones of cream to honey colored Calcite. There is a marked shift between when the lamps are viewed in natural light versus when they are softly and glowingly lit. Each rectangular lamp is 6 x 6 inches in cross-section and 15¾ and 19¼ inches tall respectively. Both are in fine condition.

Estimate: $800-$1,000

49121   ONYX WALL SCONCE

Handcrafted in Mexico

The wide band of cream to honey colored Travertine Onyx is flanked with contrasting bands of deep red to golden brown. Constructed from a single slab, this unusual wall sconce is lit by two widely separated light bulbs and when lit, the patterns spring to life. It is an impressive 25½ inches long, 8 inches wide, 4 inches deep and is wired for immediate use. Handcrafted by artisans in Mexico, the stone for this aesthetic lamp was hand selected for its bold, strong pattern. It is in very fine condition.

Estimate: $750-$1,000

49122   IRIDESCENT WHITE MOTHER-OF-PEARL SHELL TRAY

Handcrafted in the Philippines

This striking, rectangular platter gracefully and gently bows upward from all four corners; every inch covered with small rectangular pieces of mother-of-pearl shell from the Hammer Oyster. The strong, sparkling iridescence harkens to the fact that these oysters are related to pearl oysters and their name is derived from the fact that they actually do look like hammers, with the hinge of this bi-valve at the very top of the hammer head. This unique platter is in excellent condition and is 20 inches long, 11½ inches wide and sits 3 inches high.

Estimate: $800-$1,000

49123   VERY LARGE IRIDESCENT SHELL VASE

Handcrafted in the Philippines

Shimmering "rainbow" light reflects from all directions off of this very large, iridescent vase. Painstakingly handcrafted, the ceramic vase is covered by a myriad of very small, rectangular pieces of white Hammer Oyster shell that have been individually ground to match the curved form of the vase itself. Hammer Oysters (*Malleidae*) are actually a family of saltwater clams that are harvested for food and making lime in the Philippines. The iridescent white shell color has not been enhanced – it is 100% natural. An impressive example of recycling, involving many hours of patient work, the Hammer Oyster shells have been transformed to create an objet d'art. In fine condition, this sizable vase stands 26 inches high and is 15½ inches in diameter.

Estimate: $2,000-$2,500

49125 VERY LARGE ORANGE CALCITE SPHERE
Handcrafted in Mexico

The mixed orange and vanilla hues possessed by Mexican Onyx frequently evoke hidden memories of hot Summer days and deliciously cool Dreamsicle ice cream bars. The perfect sphericity and glassy luster speak to those aesthetic aspects not already subverted by the conjunction of color, internal banding and the simple pleasures of ice cream. At approximately 8 inches in diameter, this lapidary confection is not some insignificant marble left over from a children's game. It is substantial enough, to command attention from onlookers, be they small children or large. It is in excellent condition.

Estimate: $700-$1,000

49124 IRIDESCENT BLUE ABALONE SHELL VASE
Handcrafted in the Philippines

Iridescent blue-green shell from the "donkey's ear" Abalone completely covers this hand thrown ceramic vase. The shells have been sculpted so that they meld to the contours of the vase in a "crazy-quilt" pattern. The Abalones (*Haliotis asinina*) are collected for food and the shells are used to create decorative objects, usually jewelry. The iridescent quality of the shell creates a lustrous rainbow play of color which changes as the angle of view changes. The dominant shell color is a natural blue-green. A product of recycling, this "green" vase is 14½ inches high, 12 inches in diameter and is in excellent condition.

Estimate: $1,200-$1,600

49126 BRIGHT ORANGE CALCITE SPHERE
Handcrafted in Mexico

This bright orange Calcite sphere is similar in all respects to the previous lot with the exception of being slightly smaller at approximately 6 inches in diameter. Looking more like candy than stone, it is still too large to be used in a game of marbles. It is also in excellent condition.

Estimate: $500-$700

49127   TIGER-EYE BALD EAGLES ON SMOKY QUARTZ

Artist: Peter Müller

Stone Source: South Africa, Brazil & Worldwide

A mated pair of Bald Eagles are perched on a large Smoky Quartz crystal that is erupting from a white and silvery Albite & Mica base. They have been carved from chatoyant, golden Tiger-Eye and have Agate beaks, red Coral tongues, Amber eyes and snow-white Quartz heads and tails. They are gripping the smoky Quartz crystal with gold-plated sterling silver talons. One eagle has his wings outspread as if he is just landing – he is 8 inches tall, has a wingspread of 7½ inches and measures 6½ inches from beak to tail. He is being greeted by his mate, who is 6¾ inches long and 2½ inches wide. She has her beak open as if making a comment to her arriving partner. Extremely well carved, with details down to the pinfeathers, this impressive carving stands 17½ inches high, is 12¾ inches wide and over 10 inches deep, on an acrylic base. It is in fine condition and bears the artist Peter Müller's unique collection number "8975".

Estimate: $4,500-$6,500

49128   LARGE ROSE QUARTZ MACAW ON TOURMALINE

Artist: Peter Müller

Stone Source: Brazil & Worldwide

This very raucous Rose Quartz Macaw has just landed on a Tourmaline studded base and is giving everyone a piece of his mind. Squawking loudly, with his wings outspread, this very large Macaw measures an impressive 16½ inches from head to tail with a wingspan of 15 inches. The Macaw has been carved out of top grade Rose Quartz and is accented with purple Amethyst on his cheeks and on the underside of his tail. He has an orange Agate beak, black Obsidian tongue, and purple-red Rhodolite Garnet eyes. The overall sculpture stands 20 inches in height, including the acrylic stand. Peter Müller is a world renowned lapidary artist and this dramatic piece bears his unique collection #8976. It is in excellent condition.

Estimate: $7,000-$9,000

49129   RUBY MACAW COUPLE ON RED TOURMALINE BASE

Artist: Peter Müller

Stone Source: Tanzania, Brazil & Worldwide

Caught mid-conversation, these Macaws have stopped talking to look at the observer. Macaws are monogamous and mate for life, so this couple is probably talking about the kids. The Macaws bright Ruby coloration is strongly complimented by the matching red of the Tourmaline crystal. Carved out of Ruby with a smaller proportion of green Zoisite, the Macaws are resting on a Tourmaline and Quartz specimen from the Maravilla Mine of Brazil. The chatty pair of Macaws have bright Garnet eyes and beaks, and have gold plated sterling silver feet. Overall height of the sculpture is 13¾ inches, including the acrylic base. One Macaw is 11 inches from head to tail, while the other is 10 inches tall with a 7 inch wide wingspan. This pairing of colors between the carving and the mineral specimens marks the artistry of master lapidary Peter Müller and bears his unique collection #8961.

Estimate: $8,500-$10,500

49130 TOUCAN COUPLE ON POLISHED LIT ROCK CRYSTAL BASE

Artist: Peter Müller

Stone Source: South Africa, Brazil & Worldwide

This pair of colorful Toucans looks like cartoon characters but are in fact accurate representations of these comical tropical birds. Their enormous and vivid beaks have been carved out of blue green Amazonite, red Jasper, orange Calcite and black Obsidian. Their bodies are Smoky Quartz, with yellow Quartz and pink Rhodonite accents, and are detailed down to the pinfeathers. With life-like intensity, they are in conversation with their beaks open and their bright Garnet eyes flashing; they have gold plated sterling silver feet and are standing on a large, polished Quartz prism that is slightly smoky in tone. The Quartz crystal rests in a lit Granite base that can be powered by 110 or 220 volts and runs energy efficient LED lights. Both Toucans stand 8½ inches high, the overall sculpture is 17 inches high and bears Peter Müller's unique collection #8977 and is in excellent condition.

Estimate: $7,000-$9,000

49131 PUFFIN ON NEGATIVE QUARTZ BASE

Artist: Peter Müller

Stone Source: Brazil & Worldwide

This Atlantic Puffin is proudly standing on an "iceberg" of snow-white druzy Quartz, showing off his catch: a trio of translucent Chalcedony sand eels, the primary Puffin food source. Puffins have the distinct ability to hold several small fish crosswise in their bill. This skill allows them to take longer foraging trips as they can bring back more fish at a time. This life-like Puffin has been carved out of black Obsidian and white opalized Agate; his colorful beak is orange Calcite and Obsidian; and his bright eyes are Garnet, red Coral & Lapis. The large webbed feet are ideal for swimming underwater and are gold plated sterling silver. This delightful Puffin is 9½ inches from head to tail and the overall sculpture is 12¾ inches high. It bears lapidary master Peter Müller's unique collection #8975 and is in excellent condition.

Estimate: $4,000-$5,000

49132   HORSE HEAD CARVED OUT OF SMOKY QUARTZ

Artist: Peter Müller

Stone Source: Brazil & Worldwide

This stately Horse head has been carved from a single smoky Quartz prism: with alert ears that are pointed forward. The water-clear head has a brilliant polish while the flowing mane has a contrasting frosted, matte finish. The rock crystal Horse head is mounted on a gold plated sterling silver pedestal that rests on a stepped, slightly smoky, Quartz plinth. The sculpture is in excellent condition and measures just less than 9 inches high and is 5 inches wide, from the tip of the nose to the end of the mane. The fine workmanship is indicative of master lapidary artist Peter Müller and bears his unique collection #1-8750.

Estimate: $1,200-$1,800

49133   LADY'S METEORITE WATCH

Gibeon – Iron, fine octahedrite

Great Nama Land, Namibia

The face of this elegant lady's wristwatch has been fashioned from a small disc of the popular and beautiful Gibeon meteorite. Gently etched with nitric acid, the interior of this material reveals the wonderful criss-cross lattice of Widmanstätten patterns. Mounted with brass hands in a brass case stamped with Roman numerals it bears a black alligator strap and comes in a handsome keepcase.

Estimate: $250-$400

49134   LADY'S METEORITE WATCH
Gibeon – Iron, fine octahedrite
Great Nama Land, Namibia

Gibeon is among the most popular of all collectible meteorites, originating from a massive fall some thousands of years ago near the village of Gibeon in the Kalahari. Local tribesmen have used it for hundreds of years to forge blades and other tools, but here its decorative qualities are exploited in as the face of an attractive lady's watch. The watch face displays pronounced Widmanstätten patterns in the silvery metal, a fascinating lattice of criss-crossing lines in shimmering metallic shades. Mounted with brass hands in a stainless steel case, the watch was made by Starborn Creations and comes with their COA #6668.

Estimate: $200-$300

49135   CUSTOM BUCK KNIFE WITH DINOSAUR BONE HANDLE
Model CKS110
Dinosaur bone handle (probably sauropod)

Buck Knives has been producing high quality knives for over sixty years. In 1964 it introduced the folding lock-blade knife, otherwise known as the Buck Folding Hunter 110; this knife would become one of the most popular and most imitated knives in the world. The present example was constructed with a 420HC mirror polish blade, silver bolsters and cherrywood handle; a master lapidarist has removed the cherrywood, however, and replaced it on each side with a gorgeous section of polished agatized dinosaur bone from the famed Morrison formation in Utah. The earthy shades of black, blue-gray and brown are dashed through with deep vibrant red, and the lovely orbicular patterning represents the tiny intricate cellular arrangement of tubular branching 'Haversian Canals' that veined the interior of the dinosaur's skeleton; these canals originally housed blood vessels and nerve cells but during the process of fossilization, under certain conditions, they can become filled with a beautiful colorful agate, creating the highly aesthetic effect seen here. The blade measures 3⅝ inches and the handle 4⅞ inches, and comes with a woolen pouch, leather holster and COA.

Estimate: $1,800-$2,400

49136 TRANSLUCENT BLUE CHALCEDONY BOX
Handcrafted in Italy
Stone source: South Africa

This blue Chalcedony box has been fashioned from a solid block of top-grade material from the Ysterputs Farm on the South African-Namibian border region, the only source for this wonderful pastel blue stone. Solid pieces of this stone, with this depth of color, marks it as being from an earlier mining period, and indeed this prize material had long been in the inventory of an Idar Oberstein lapidary master carver. He passed it on to the Italian artisan who created this fine translucent box with striking "cloud" and "ring" patterns. This one-of-a-kind box measures 3.54 x 5.12 inches (9 x 13 cm), has gold plated brass furniture and is in excellent condition.
Estimate: $1,600-$2,000

49137 ROYAL BLUE LAPIS BOX
Handcrafted in Italy
Stone source: Afghanistan

Royal blue Lapis has a deep, rich coloration that only comes from the mines of Afghanistan: the premier world locality. In fact, before the Russian invasion of Afghanistan, the country's currency was backed by a substantial quantity of top grade Lapis. The white Calcite veins and the sprinkling of golden Pyrite crystals indicate that this is natural, untreated material. The Italian lapidary master has matched the patterning of each side of the box with the top, so there is a seamless transition. In excellent condition, this gemstone box features a Black Onyx interior, gold plated furniture and measures 3.9 x 5.9 inches (15 x 10 cm).
Estimate: $2,000-$2,750

49138   LARGE "SPAGHETTI" BOX
Handcrafted in Italy
Stone source: Worldwide

This striking tessellated box has been crafted by a master Italian lapidary whose skill is such that there are virtually no gaps in the inlay work. It has earned the name "spaghetti" because it resembles pieces of spaghetti that have been pieced together to form a solid pattern. A riot of color has been created by a vast array of stones from around the world: Amazonite from Russia, Rhodochrosite from Argentina, Malachite from Congo, Blue Chalcedony from Namibia, Picture Jasper from Utah, Fossil Stromatolite from Bolivia, Lapis from Afghanistan, Amethyst from Brazil, Tiger-Eye from South Africa, Sodalite from Namibia, Aventurine from India, Labradorite from Madagascar, and Tiger-Iron from Australia, as well as numerous world-wide Jaspers, Onyx, Granites and Rhyolites. In excellent condition, this sizable box measures 4.7 x 7.9 inches (20 x 12 cm), has gold plated brass furniture and a Black Onyx interior.
Estimate: $2,500-$3,000

49139   IMPRESSIVE LARGE RHODOCHROSITE BOX
Handcrafted in Italy
Stone source: Argentina

One of the largest, if not the largest, Rhodochrosite box created by an Italian lapidary master. Argentine Rhodochrosite from the Catamarca Province is renowned worldwide and is the only source of this unique lapidary material. The rich pink to raspberry pink Rhodochrosite has elaborate "flower" patterning caused by a multiplicity of stalactites growing together over several millennia. An uncommonly large Rhodochrosite stalactite was needed to create this box. Measuring a stately 7.9 x 11.8 x 3.9 inches (20 x 30 x 10 cm), the patterns on the top flow impeccably down each side, with flawlessly executed matching. This unique box is not to be repeated, as the mine is no longer producing material of this size or caliber. It is in excellent condition.
Estimate: $12,500-$15,000

49140   SIZABLE "BULL'S-EYE" MALACHITE BOX

Handcrafted in Italy

Stone source: Democratic Republic of Congo

Malachite "bull's-eyes" are created by slicing a stalactite to reveal its interior patterning. "Bull's-eyes" with strong patterning are highly prized. This magnificent box has a total of six such large "bull's-eyes": two on the lid and one on each side. The flawless execution by the master Italian lapidary has created the illusion of a seamless block of Malachite with incredible patterning – the inlay seams are literally invisible. The sides of the box are matched with the lid to the point where the "bull's-eyes" actually wrap up from the sides onto the lid. A truly one-of-a-kind box, it has gold plated brass furniture, Black Onyx interior and is in excellent condition. It measures an impressive 9.45 x 6.3 inches (24 x 16 cm).

Estimate: $7,000-$8,500

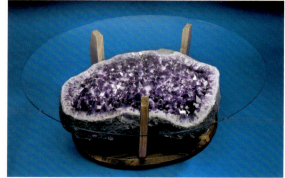

49141   AMETHYST COFFEE TABLE

Rio Grande do Sul, South Region, Brazil

The centerpiece of this elegant little table is a fine shallow amethyst geode boasting a dense carpet of good blocky crystals, boasting a fine deep purple coloring. The crystals protrude above the sliced and hand-polished edge of the geode denoting an unusually painstaking craftsmanship. This conjunction of artisanal and natural beauty is framed by three curved walnut supports from an oval base, and viewed through a large oval glass top 37⅞ x 28 inches; at 16 inches high it is a practical, unusual and above all beautiful furnishing piece.

Estimate: $1,800-$2,400

49142 OCTAGONAL FOSSIL MARBLE TABLETOP

Orthoceras sp., Agoniatites sp.
Devonian
Sahara Desert, near Talmud, Morocco

At the center of this fine tabletop is a good specimen of the Agoniatites ammonite, its remains having been calcified to an almost pure white and the chambers filled with the tan, gray and black shades characteristic of marble from this region of North Africa. Bound in a thin line of brass it is radiated by further brass banding to segment the tabletop into eight, each comprised of Devonian marble and studded with the shells of more ammonites and the cone-like Orthoceras, on a ground composed of lovely warm tones of earthy brown and red. At 31 inches wide it can be presented with equal impact as a highly unusual tabletop or a beautiful wall plaque.

Estimate: $1,200-$1,500

49143   UNUSUAL FOSSIL MARBLE TABLETOP

Orthoceras sp., Agoniatites sp.
Devonian
Sahara Desert, near Talmud, Morocco

One thinks one knows the character of the Devonian fossil marble from North Africa and then a piece like this comes along. Cut from a single large piece of 400 million year old fossiliferous marble it boasts a striking Ammonite shell near the centre, vividly and naturally colored in white and gray. This is a fine if familiar feature of marble from this region; less common, however, is the lovely wavy patterning of the background, instantly evocative of the sea shore. In fact, in shades of red and brown with speckled black patterning, it probably represents the natural undulations of the ancient ocean floor and the effect is one of great natural aesthetic beauty, further dotted with the ghostly remains of the cone-shaped Orthoceras belemnite. With sloping beveled edges this unique and beautiful tabletop measures 39¼ x 21¾ inches.

Estimate: $1,400-$1,800

49144   LARGE FOSSIL MARBLE TABLETOP
Orthoceras sp., Agoniatites sp.
Devonian
Sahara Desert, near Talmud, Morocco
This massive slab of fossiliferous seabed marble has been cut
and polished from a single block and teems with a wonderful
array of earthy shades and swirling patterns, from which
emerge as though from the distant past the remains of the
ancient ocean's denizens. Ammonites and Orthoceras are
represented in vivid contrasting shades of white and gray,
creating a beautiful natural canvas that makes for an immediately
striking furnishing piece, polished to a lustrous smoothness
with a curved bevel to the edge, 55 x 31½ inches.
Estimate: $1,800-$2,400

49145   LARGE LABRADORITE MOSAIC TABLETOP
Madagascar
Labradorite is a highly sought-after mineral, for the optical
phenomenon known as labradorescence. Twinning on a
microscopic level reflects light in such a way that the sheets of
golden green and electric blue seem to shimmer just below the
surface of the stone. This lovely tabletop has been fashioned from
numerous sections of the mineral and several of them exhibit this
captivating characteristic, enhanced by the high polish that has
been applied to the lustrous surface. An unusual and immediately
striking furnishing piece, it measures 53¾ x 29 inches.
Estimate: $6,000-$7,500

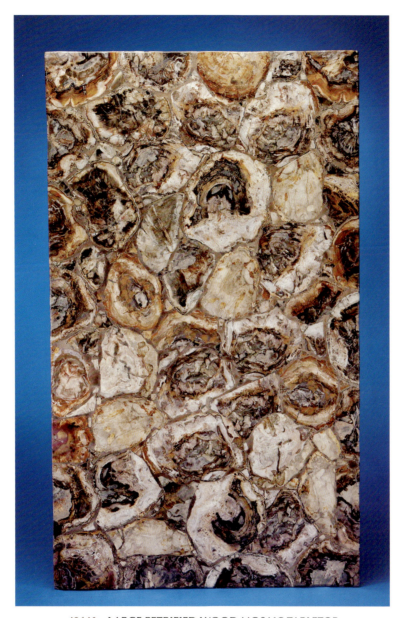

49146   LARGE PETRIFIED WOOD MOSAIC TABLETOP
Podocarpus sp.
Triassic
Mahajanga, Madagascar

This large tabletop has been created from several beautiful slices of ancient Gondwanan conifer from the island of Madagascar. A locale famed for the abundance of its fossil and mineral specimens, its wood is amongst the most beautifully mineral-replaced in the world. The polished surface of the tabletop swirls with patterns conforming to the original cellular structure of the trees, but in a riot of beautifully pale earthy colors as a result of millions of years of mineral replacement; brown, tan and cream shades are highlighted by a soft gray-blue and streaks of orange. A lovely furnishing piece, it measures 55 x 32½ inches.

Estimate: $5,500-$6,500

49147 ELEPHANT PAIR BRONZE
Artist: Mark Hopkins – #664 of 750
This finely detailed bust of a pair of African Elephants was sculpted in the early 1960's. With their trunks entwined the pose of mother and child evokes a lifelike moment of closeness and stands about 16¼ inches high from a simulated rocky base.
Estimate: $800-$1,500

49148 AFRICAN LION BRONZE
Antoine Louis Barye
This beautiful bronze of a reclining male Lion was executed in 1957 by Antoine Louis Barye, an artist known for his African animal bronzes. It boasts excellent detail and mounted on a dark gray marble base it measures 11¼ inches long and 6⅜ inches high.
Estimate: $750-$1,100

49149 CAPE BUFFALO BRONZE
Antoine Louis Barye
This very handsome Cape Buffalo bronze was sculpted in 1958. The Cape Buffalo is one of Africa's Big 5 Big Game animals and can be very dangerous when wounded. Mounted on a deep bluish-black marble base it measures 14⅜ inches wide and stands 9¼ inches high.
Estimate: $800-$1,200

49150   37 FINE NEOLITHIC GEM POINTS
3,000-6,000 B.P.
Sahara Desert
These beautifully colored gem points are finely knapped and made from various varieties of chert, chalcedony, jasper, quartzite, and flint. Years of exposure to the intense gamma radiation of the North African sun have given them a rich patina combined with the light burnished finish created by windblown sand polishing, displayed in a 16¼ x 12¼ inch Riker mount.
Estimate: $2,500-$3,000

49151   25 FINE NEOLITHIC GEM POINTS
3,000-6,000 B.P.
Sahara Desert
Similar to the previous lot, these 25 various colored gem points are finely knapped and expertly fashioned, displaying a variety of notched shoulders, stems, and serrations. Thousands of years in the burning desert sun and the action of the hot and sand-heavy Saharan winds have given them a lovely burnished luster, displayed in a 16¼ x 12¼ inch Riker mount.
Estimate: $1,800-$2,400

49152   25 FINE NEOLITHIC GEM POINTS
3,000-6,000 B.P.
Sahara Desert
What is now the barren Sahara was once an area rich in plant and animal life along the coastal plains of North Africa. These were rich hunting grounds for our ancestors, the local natives, and this collection of points is a fine representation of the weapons they used to take down the wildlife they hunted for food, nicely displayed in a 16¼ x 12¼ inch Riker mount.
Estimate: $1,800-$2,400

49153   FINE NEWTON FALLS POINT
Early to Middle Archaic – 8,000-5,000
Newton Falls, Ohio
This superb G-9 point has a beautifully bright and smooth patina and shows excellent quality workmanship. Finely knapped from Baileys chert it exhibits good overall patination and mineralization and measures 2⅞ x 1 inch with a Baker COA.
Estimate: $400-$650

49154   FINE HARDIN POINT
Early Archaic – 8,500-6,000 B.P.
Jersey co., Illinois
This is a very old and large dart/knife finely fashioned from Burlington chert. The blade has been re-sharpened once which created slightly beveled cutting edges lightly reducing the size. It measures 3¹³⁄₁₆ x 1⁷⁄₁₆ inches and is accompanied by a Gregory Perino COA.
Estimate: $700-$1,000

49157   DALTON POINT

Late Paleo-Indian -10,500 -9,000 B.P.
Missouri

The Dalton Point is a variant of the classic Clovis Point, bi-facially worked with a hollow base rather than the fishtail outline. It is a feature of the Dalton culture which emerged across the American southwest at the end of the Paleo-Indian Period over 10,000 years ago. The present G-8 example was made from Burlington Chert and boasts good overall patination and mineralization, measuring 3¼ x ¹⁵⁄₁₆ inches with a Baker COA.

Provenance: Terry Allen Collection
Estimate: $900-$1,200

49155   HUGE DOVETAIL POINT

Early Archaic – 8,000-7,500 B.P.
Barren, Kentucky

This is a huge point measuring 4½ x 1¹¹⁄₁₆ inches and was made from either Sainte Genevieve chert or hornstone. Known also as Plevna in the south and St. Charles points in the Midwest, it is believed to be at least 7,500 years old, based on excavations at the Tellico Reservoir in Eastern Tennessee where beveled points were found to pre-date the Kirk Cornered Notch Horizon. This fine example displays high quality workmanship with a smooth patina and a chip to the tip that appears to be prehistoric, accompanied by a Jerry Dickey COA.

Provenance: Bill Wagner, James Osman Collections
Estimate: $1,200-$1,800

49156   LARGE ETLEY SPEARPOINT

Late Archaic – 3,000-5,000 B.P.
Stanton, Franklin co., Missouri

Etley Points are closely associated with the Titterington Phase of the lower Illinois Valley and is often found in association with the Wadlow, Smith, Sedalia and other contemporary types of point. The present example was expertly knapped from Burlington chert and boasts a fine patina, 5⁵⁄₁₆ x 1⅜ inches with collector's inscription, provenance label and Jerry Dickey COA.

Provenance: Charlie Wiesbecker, Marion Kent, Ron Hall Collections
Estimate: $800-$1,200

49158   CAMPO DEL CIELO METEORITE — NATURAL SCULPTURE FROM OUTER SPACE — FEATURED ON THE SCIENCE CHANNEL'S "METEORITE MEN"

Iron, coarse octahedrite

Gran Chaco, Argentina

From the Macovich Collection of Meteorites – the most renowned collection of aesthetic iron meteorites in the world – comes what is not only among the most unusual meteorites from Argentina's Campo del Cielo meteorite shower, it's among the more aesthetic iron meteorites period. Meteorites almost never look like the sculptural example offered here which exhibits a most unusual one-inch deep crevasse running its length. Campo del Cielo ("Valley of the Sky") meteorites were first written about in 1576 by Spanish explorers when their unearthly origin had yet to be understood. A meteorite from Campo del Cielo was the first large meteorite displayed at the British Museum of Natural History, and several large "Campo" masses can be found today in the finest museums throughout the world. While the meteorite now offered also features a rare and sought-after naturally formed hole (unseen in the accompanying image), the defining characteristic of this flanged specimen is the shallow fissure that runs along its length – a feature rarely documented. Broad rippled crests accentuate this meteorite's pewter-to-platinum patina. Compelling from any angle in any orientation, this offering embodies every ideal of splendor and wonder of an unconventionally shaped iron meteorite. Accompanied by a custom armature from which it can readily be removed, this meteorite was featured on an episode of the Science Channel's "Meteorite Men." A copy of the program accompanies this lot, as does a Macovich Collection provenance. 328 x 366 x 209 mm (13 x 14½ x 8¼ inches) and 46.2 kilograms (101.75 pounds)

Estimate: $22,500-$30,000

49159   CAMPO DEL CIELO — CLASSIC IRON METEORITE
Iron, coarse octahedrite
Gran Chaco, Argentina

About 4000 years ago; a giant iron meteor weighing over 100 tons, impacted a region of Argentina. This event was likely witnessed by natives in the area and passed down in oral tradition until it was reported to the Spaniards in the 1500's that large chunks of iron in the area had originally "fallen from heaven." The oral tradition is probably what gave the region its name; "Campo del Cielo" or "Valley of the Sky." This specimen is a classic example from the famous region; it features gently undulating contours and is a rough hourglass shape when viewed from one side. This meteorite features a glossy dark gray gun-metal patina with speckles of rust-orange across the surface. This classic specimen measures 10½ x 3½ x 3½ inches, weighing 15 lbs 13 ounces, sits snuggly on a custom display stand.

Estimate: $950-$1,250

49160   CAMPO DEL CIELO — COMPLETE IRON METEORITE
Iron, coarse octahedrite
Gran Chaco, Argentina

With its metallic shard-like appearance and the strange thumbprint-like impressions (regmaglypts) covering its surface; this unearthly natural sculpture is unmistakably extraterrestrial in origin. Discovered in the "Valley Of The Sky" in Argentina, this meteorite was part of a much larger impact that occurred over 4000 years ago. The warm patina and hints of shining iron lend it an incomparable character, tiny speckles of rust coat its flanks and hints to the ancient age of the specimen. Sitting on a custom-made stand, this fine meteorite measures 8 x 5½ x 3 inches and weighs 12 lbs 13 ounces.

Estimate: $850-$1,200

49161 CAMPO DEL CIELO — NATURAL SCULPTURE

Iron, coarse octahedrite
Gran Chaco, Argentina

Iron meteorites originate from the molten core of what were planetary-sized bodies between Mars and Jupiter during the formation of the solar system. Such *plantetoids* (large unstable planetary bodies) broke apart approximately 4.5 billion years ago whose remnants are today referred to as the asteroid belt – which is from where this, and most other meteorites, originate. The present specimen features a surface of smooth metallic contours and thumb-print sized regmaglypt impressions. It displays a dark gunmetal patina and comes complete with a custom stand, measuring 6 x 4 x 3 inches and weighs 12 lbs 2 ounces.
Estimate: $850-$1,200

49162 SIKHOTE-ALIN — FASCINATING EXAMPLE FROM THE LARGEST METEORITE SHOWER SINCE THE DAWN OF CIVILIZATION

Iron, coarse octahedrite
Maritime Territory, Siberia

This splendid meteorite originates from one of the most frightening phenomena ever experienced. It arrived on Earth on February 12, 1947 where it was part of the largest meteorite shower of the last several thousand years. Thousands of small specimens broke up in the upper atmosphere, and when a large mass exploded a few miles above Earth's surface, tons of shrapnel was sent hurtling onto the snowy terrain below. The local populace was terrified; from a distance of fifty miles it appeared the sky was on fire. Craters were created, trees were impaled, yet no one was injured as the impact area was unpopulated. This surprisingly heavy specimen exhibits twisting folds and deep striations on all faces except one – where the telltale thumbprints of the exterior surface of a meteorite are in evidence. This is undoubtedly from a much larger mass which exploded in the lower atmosphere – perhaps the largest mass previously referred to – as both the internal and external surface of this meteorite are visible. Had this meteorite split apart during the initial phase of its descent, the entire meteorite would be covered with the fine flight markings, but that's not the case. Testament to the monumental shearing force exerted on a large meteorite, this fascinating specimen is naturally burnished in a lustrous gunmetal patina with bronze accents. This is an exceptional example of a cataclysmic event frozen in time, from the most terrifying meteorite shower of modern times. From the Macovich Collection of Meteorites, the finest collection of aesthetic iron meteorites in the world. 158 x 111 x 123 mm (6¼ x 4½ x 4¾ inches) and 4,275 grams (9.5 pounds).
Estimate: $5,500-$7,000

49163 SIKHOTE-ALIN — AESTHETIC IRON METEORITE FROM THE LARGEST METEORITE SHOWER IN THE PAST SEVERAL THOUSAND YEARS

Iron, coarse octahedrite

Maritime Territory, Siberia, Russia

Similar to the previous lot, this sculptural example also originates from the unimaginably massive Siberian meteorite shower of February 1947. The forces exerted on this object as it rocketed through Earth's atmosphere are amply evident: blanketed with fusion crust and scores of fresh *regmaglypts* (the aerodynamic thumbprints which result from its fiery plunge through Earth's atmosphere), the largely flat backside of this wing-shaped meteorite is proof of it having split along a crystalline plane in the upper atmosphere as well as being *oriented*, a sought-after characteristic: it descended through the atmosphere without the typical spinning and tumbling of most meteorites as revealed by the smooth surface character of the reverse. Burnished in a bright patina with chrome highlights and accompanied by a custom armature, this unusual and artfully sculpted meteorite is from the most frightening meteorite shower of modern times. 155 x 129 x 63 mm (6 x 5 x 2½ inches) and 1849 grams (4 pounds).

Provenance: Macovich Collection

Estimate: $3,500-$4,500

49164 GIBEON METEORITE END PIECE — INTERNAL AND EXTERNAL CHARACTER REVEALED IN A SUPERB IRON METEORITE

Iron, fine octahedrite

Great Nama Land, Namibia

Recovered from the edge of the Kalahari Desert, Gibeon iron meteorites are the bounty of a huge meteorite shower that occurred thousands of years ago when an enormous iron mass (or masses) fragmented upon impact with Earth's atmosphere. This select example exhibits both the internal structure and external character of an iron meteorite to exquisite effect. The exterior surface of this meteorite is draped in a muted gunmetal patina, and several concavities – the likes of which are seen on only the best Gibeon meteorites – are in ample evidence. Dramatically contrasting with its rich external surface, the internal crystalline structure of this specimen bedazzles. This meteorite originated from a planetary body that broke apart (whose fragments are part of the asteroid belt). Upon splitting open, there was little that the hot metallic core could transfer it's heat to in the vacuum of space, so the material stayed somewhat warm, in the absolute cold, for millions of years providing sufficient time for nickel-iron crystals to form. As there is no other environment other than the vacuum of space that provides such long cooling curves, the presence of this latticework, referred to as a *Widmanstätten pattern*, is diagnostic in the identification of a meteorite. This specimen also contains *Neumann bands*, the result of a violent impact and consequent shocking of material in space and *troilite* (iron sulfide) inclusions – another signature hallmark of Gibeon meteorites. This is a superlative representation of the internal and external structure of an iron meteorite. 159 x 99 x 37 mm (6¼ x 4 x 1½ inches) and 1627 grams (3.5 pounds).

Provenance: Macovich Collection of Meteorites

Estimate: $2,500-$3,500

49165   GIBEON METEORITE — COMPLETE SLICE
Iron, fine octahedrite
Great Nama Land, Namibia
Similar to the previous lot, millions of years are required for the alloys that chiefly comprise iron meteorites to crystallize, a feature that is diagnostic in the identification of an iron meteorite, and evident in the current offering to fantastic effect. This complete slice exhibits a complexly woven Widmanstätten structure and a gently winding rim of the meteorite's external surface. The shimmering matrix is accented with signature iron sulfide inclusions. 175 x 97 x 3 mm (7 x 4 x ⅛ inches) and 276 grams.
Estimate: $500-$700

49166   CANYON DIABLO — NATURAL, PRIMITIVE TABLETOP SCULPTURE FROM THE BEST PRESERVED METEORITE CRATER ON EARTH
Iron, coarse octahedrite
Meteor Crater, Coconino County, Arizona

Like most meteorites, the present specimen originated in the asteroid belt, but approximately 45,000 years ago this specimen was part of an errant asteroid that plowed into the Arizona desert with the force of more than 100 atomic bombs. While fragments were ejected more than 11 miles away from the point of impact, the main mass vaporized, creating the most famous and best preserved meteorite crater in the world, the renowned "Meteor Crater" near Winslow, Arizona, nearly one mile across and 600 feet deep. Canyon Diablo ("Canyon of the Devil") is the quintessential American meteorite, prized by museums and private collectors everywhere, and this is a superb tabletop example. Blanketed in a platinum to smoky patina and seemingly bowed to the right with radiating soft ridges, a deep socket is seen in the lower left, undoubtedly where a graphite nodule had been ejected from the nickel-iron mass during impact.

It was in 1903 that businessman Daniel M. Barringer reasoned that the suspicious crater in the desert floor had to have been created by an enormous mass weighing millions of tons and he believed this mass, worth a fortune in iron and nickel, lay under the crater's base. Barringer filed a mining claim on the site that later became known as "Barringer's Crater." A small fortune was spent on drilling that went on for decades and no large mass was ever found. Unfortunately for Barringer, an asteroid far smaller than what he imagined would possess sufficient energy to blow such a huge hole in the desert floor... and it would generate enough heat to vaporize much of its mass. In effect, the mass that Barringer spent the last thirty years of his life searching for didn't exist. But this select example of extraterrestrial Americana does, and Meteor Crater, which is still owned by the Barringer family, is still a sight to behold. 179 x 144 x 89 mm (7 x 5½ x 3½ inches) and 5999 grams (13.2 pounds).
Estimate: $4,000-$5,000

49167 CANYON DIABLO — SCULPTURAL SPICULAR METEORITE FROM THE "CANYON OF THE DEVIL"

Iron, coarse octahedrite

Meteor Crater, Coconino County, Arizona

Similar to the previous lot, this palm-size meteorite is a pocketful of wonder. Featuring unusually soft edges and numerous ridges in a muted steel patina, this is an engaging example of a Canyon Diablo, the quintessential American meteorite. Originating from an impact that produced a crater one mile across and six hundred feet deep, Canyon Diablos are highly sought after and the source material is now nearly depleted. Spicules like the current offering were flung 45,000 years ago as far as 11 miles following the asteroid's impact. 108 x 67 x 39 mm (4¼ x 2½ x 1½ inches) and 235.3 grams (½ pound).

Estimate: $400-$500

49168 LARGE AND UNUSUAL MUONIONALUSTA END SECTION

Fine (IVA) octahedrite

Kiruna, Norrbotten, Northern Sweden

Although no-one has so far located its impact crater, the Muonionalusta meteorite is believed to have fallen over 800,000 years ago somewhere in the Arctic Circle. Glacial action carried parts of the fall to northern Sweden, where they were first recorded in 1906; the geological conditions and Sweden's legislative restrictions on metal detectors make them extremely difficult to recover, but this excellent example shows that they are well worth the effort. Exhibiting the best of both worlds, it is a large flat end piece, with a great expanse of fusion crust and an etched inner face, exposing the fascinating silvery Widmanstätten patterns of latticed nickel-iron kamacite and taenite. Most remarkable, however, is a distinct line across the sliced face, bordered by a dense concentration of particularly fine stress lines: this is the border between two distinct crystal structures resulting from an incredibly high impact collision between two pieces of the original mass somewhere out in space. It is a highly unusual feature, and only adds to the appeal and fascination of an already excellent specimen, 12 x 9⅞ x 2¼ inches, and weighing 26 lb 7 oz with a metal display stand.

Estimate: $8,500-$10,000

LOVINA

Iron, ataxite (ungrouped)
Lovina Beach, Bali, Indonesia

49169   NOTABLE OFFERING OF THE INCOMPARABLE LOVINA METEORITE — COMPLETE SLICE FROM A UNIQUE MINERAL SPECIMEN AND ONLY METEORITE TO EXHIBIT LARGE PYRAMIDAL STRUCTURES

Why this specimen was withdrawn from our previous sale, and its triumphal return

In December 2009, two meteorite researchers wondered if Lovina – certified by scientists as a meteorite in 2008 – might not be a meteorite after all, but instead be a highly exotic form of oxidized slag. Further research into Lovina's origins immediately commenced, but the results were not available prior to our January sale, and so the specimen was pulled from the offering. This past February, the world's foremost expert in iron meteorites, Dr. John Wasson, announced the results of his new research. "I am convinced Lovina is a meteorite; every single element is within the range commonly encountered in iron meteorites. Metals that have been made by man will *always* differ from meteorites in terms of several elements and element ratios." Dr. Wasson's findings were endorsed by the scientists who prompted the new investigation, and Wasson's determination reaffirmed Lovina's standing as a singularly unique meteorite. Months later Wasson stated he was still puzzled by the object which he thought was most likely a meteorite. Heritage Auction Galleries is honored to be able to offer a select complete slice from what is inarguably one of the most exotic metallic objects on Earth. The unabridged January 2010 catalog description follows.

From Lovina Beach, Bali, Indonesia, comes the meteorite for which museums and private collectors are today clamoring. Scarce and only recently available, this is the first public offering of Lovina – what scientists have described as the single most unique iron meteorite. In terms of its external structure, Lovina is the only meteorite with pyramids. In terms of its internal structure, Lovina is the only iron meteorite to reveal an organized, lattice-like matrix of inclusions and vugs. In addition, Lovina is also one of a handful of underwater meteorite finds, and is the only meteorite find recovered from a body of water where there was not an additional meteorite from the same event first recovered from the shoreline.

It was in 1981 that a 13-year-old Canadian boy recovered an unusual metallic rock from the tropical Balinese shallows while searching for shells at Lovina Beach. He knew nothing about meteorites – had no idea at all what they looked like – but this did not prevent him from earnestly reporting to his family that he found a rock from outer space. Extremely exotic, the heavy rock looked nothing like any meteorite ever seen. With two-dozen one-inch metallic pyramids perched on

Pictured here is the main mass of Lovina from which the slice now offered originates. The pyramidal structures — the finest example of tetrataenite — will be preserved intact for anticipated museum acquisition.

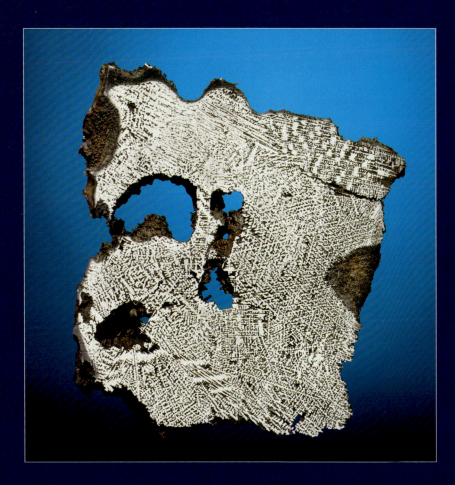

a coral-like base, this would easily have to be the most unusually shaped meteorite to exist. As the years went by, the boy was entirely content to hold onto his find. He returned to Canada with his family, kept his rock in a tackle box and became a miner.

In 2008, he was introduced to meteorite researchers at Western Ontario University. When the rock's extraterrestrial origin was confirmed, the owner was nonplussed and later conveyed, "Over all these years, I've never had as much faith in anything as this being a meteorite."

With its 34.5% nickel content, Lovina has the 4th largest nickel concentration of any meteorite, which intrinsically makes it among the most valuable meteorites per unit weight. In a curious anecdotal twist, long before he was informed of his meteorite's mineralogy, the young boy who found the meteorite with one of the greatest concentrations of nickel worked as a young man at one of *Earth's* largest concentrations of nickel – in a nickel mine in Sudbury, Ontario.

The extraordinary *ziggurat* (stepped pyramidal) structures are partially the result of the meteorite being rich in tetrataenite – a polymorph of taenite, but with nearly three times the nickel content. Troilite inclusions and vugs arrayed in a novel latticework also promoted ziggurat growth. As a result of its mineralogy, this meteorite was selectively resistant to the oxidizing effect of the tropical waters in which it was immersed for centuries. In sum, the pyramidal structures are the result of several exotic attributes of the meteorite and circumstances (falling in the wave-swept shallows of a tropical ocean and anchoring to a terrestrial rock) that serendipitously came together.

The complete slice offered here, one of only eleven complete slices, reveals a plentitude of vugs and inclusions and is accented by three natural holes, artifacts of weathering in tropical waters. Said Marlin Cilz of the Montana Meteorite Laboratory (which has prepared specimens for the American Museum of Natural History (New York), The Natural History Museum (London) and countless other institutions, "Lovina is the most bizarre, unreal meteorite I've ever seen in 30 years." For the sophisticated collector, this is an exceptional representation of what will forever be one of the more remarkable meteorites – and one that can grace only a limited number of collections. Lovina weighed less than eleven pounds and a five-pound section containing the pyramidal structures was removed in anticipation of it becoming a museum centerpiece. This lot comes accompanied by a copy of its abstract in Lunar and Planetary Science (XXXIX) and a high res image of the entire mass. 42 x 46 x 3 mm (1¾ x 1¾ x ⅛ inches) and 31.53 grams.

Provenance: Macovich Collection of Meteorites – the world's finest collection of aesthetic iron meteorites.

Estimate: $8,500-$9,500

49170 FULL SLICE OF A MOON ROCK
NWA 2995 (NWA=Northwest Africa)
Lunar Feldspathic Breccia
Lunar Meteorite with a Total Known Weight of 538 grams
Algeria; Discovered 2005

This specimen is a full slice of a beautiful, very fresh 538 gram complete individual. Its mineralogy is that of a lunar feldspathic fragmental breccia that contains many FHT (Feldspathic Highlands Terrain) fine-grained rock types including norite, olivine basalt, gabbro and others. This meteorite comes from the lunar highlands which cover 84% of the Moon's surface. This type of lunar meteorite is produced by shock-welding lunar soil – Shock-welding is caused by the impact of a large meteorite nearby which, much like a nuclear weapon, releases massive amounts of heat energy (thermal radiation) and shock waves. Shock-welding occurs when the impact is far enough away that no direct melting occurs, and only the massive shock wave crushes and compresses the rock or regolith (lunar surface soil) together, creating a new rock, very much like making a snowball by squeezing the snow between one's hands. The incredible pressures generated by these nuclear weapon-strength impacts regularly produced very large zones of shock-welded material which, then, had to be blasted into space by an even larger impact in order to get to Earth. This particular lunar meteorite is composed of multiple types of rock from at least four generations of impact events which successively blasted the lunar surface rock apart and re-welded it into a new breccia – repeated at least four times. There is some impact or thermal melting as well as shock-melting in pockets and veins. The source of the material for the breccia was not surface soil, but deeper fragmented lunar soil with no exposure to the solar wind or cosmic rays. Because the source rocks for the lunar soil are from the highlands, only the oldest and more common lunar rock types are usually represented with ages of approximately 4.2 – 4.3 billion years old. This gorgeous slice has the added attraction of being virtually indistinguishable from an actual Apollo Mission moon rock with its large white anorthosite and greenish gabbroic fragments being offset by the dark gray and black background matrix. It also has a rind of desirable fusion crust around the entire edge. A superb, museum-worthy, eye-catching lunar meteorite! This slice has a very large surface area for the weight and measures 43.3 x 31.0 x 1.6 mm thick (1¾ x 1¼ x ¹⁄₁₆ inches) and weighs 4.26 grams.
Estimate: $7,000-$8,000

49171   PART SLICE OF A MOON ROCK
NWA 2995 (NWA=Northwest Africa)
Lunar Feldspathic Breccia
Lunar Meteorite with a Total Known Weight of 538 grams
Algeria – Found 2005
Similar to the previous lot, though smaller, measuring 28.7 x 20.4 x 1.6 mm thick (1⅛ x ⅞ x ⅝ inches) and weighs 2.39 grams.
Estimate: $4,000-$4,500

49172 A SLICE OF A MARTIAN METEORITE

DAG 1037, Basaltic Shergottite
Dar al Gani, Sahara Desert, Libya
Discovered 1999

This meteorite, identified and described in The Meteoritical Bulletin in 2004, is probably one of the most important Martian meteorites ever discovered because it contains large shock-melt veins, gas vesicles, and shock-altered olivine, indicating that it was very close to, if not precisely at, the impact site of the asteroid believed to be the source of most of the Martian meteorites known. The basalt (iron and magnesium-rich cooled lava) composition of this meteorite proves that there was active vulcanism on Mars 474 million years ago which means that Mars was not a dead planet like the Moon. Indeed, the early Martian atmosphere was much thicker, warmer, wetter and possibly capable of sustaining life! The lovely green color is reminiscent of fine spinach jade with black, shock-altered olivine crystals pleasingly interspersed throughout the matrix. A large black shock-melt vein runs diagonally across the edge of the slice and has numerous gas vesicles filled with micro crystals. Shock-melting and veins are caused by huge shock waves or gravitational shear, where solid rock instantly liquefies, in veins where the greatest stresses build up within a rock body, during a cataclysmic event such as a meteoroid/asteroid impact. This attractive specimen measures 32 x 23 x 1.5 mm thick (1¼ x ⅞ x ⅝ inches) and weighs 1.81 grams.

Estimate: $2,000-$2,750

49173 METEORITE BELIEVED TO BE FROM THE PLANET MERCURY — AN ANGRITE

NWA 3164
Angrite
Morocco; Discovered 2004

Angrites are an exceptionally rare type of achondrite meteorite and are from a parent body much closer to the Sun than Earth. They were formed as the result of a very large impact which penetrated to the mantle of the parent body and mixed crust and mantle materials along with the impact body, thought to be a very large iron meteorite, resulting in the unique characteristics that only Angrites possess. Several mineralogical and structural characteristics point to Mercury as the origin for the Angrites, but the evidence is insufficient to prove beyond a reasonable doubt that Mercury is the parent body. Thus, we can only hope that more of these exotic and extremely rare meteorites are found so that the source body can one day be definitively identified. Angrites are rarer than meteorites from the Moon or Mars and are likely the rarest and most desired class of planetary meteorite.

The present specimen represented here is a full slice from a complete individual, measuring 43.8 x 39.2 x 2.5 mm thick (1⅝ x 1½ x ⅛ inches) and weighing 10.06 grams. It is characterized by large polygonal grains of anorthite (purplish-brown), olivine (dark green), shocked olivine (black) and spinel (yellow-orange) contained in a fine-grained matrix. This meteorite is quite beautiful in thin sections or reflected light with the orange colored grains of spinel standing out in sharp contrast to the other minerals, and there is a striking schiller effect from the dark green olivine crystals as the slice is rotated in the light.

Estimate: $2,600-$3,000

49174 UNCOMMONLY LARGE STONY METEORITE

NWA – Chondrite
Northern Sahara

One of the most abundant sources of meteorites outside of the Antarctic is the Sahara Desert, where the dry even weather has provided the perfect conditions for these rocks from the sky to lie undisturbed and undamaged for thousands of years until they are collected by the nomadic Berbers of the region. Most are chondrites, or stony meteorites, the most abundant type of meteorite found on Earth (comprising approximately 80%) and given their profusion many examples from this region remain unclassified. This is just such an example, and a fine one at that: it features a splendidly varied and textured fusion crust with one face almost entirely flat, while other areas are richly dimpled with a concavity of excellent thumbprint-sized regmaglypts. In addition one "corner" has been sliced off and the face polished to provide a view of the interior structure, its attractive patterning reminiscent of agatized dinosaur bone. This fine-sized specimen, among the largest stone meteorite ever offered at public auction, weighs in at around 80 lb and measures approximately 17 x 11½ x 9 inches. Presented on a custom metal display stand measuring 23⅝ inches high overall.

Estimate: $9,500-$12,000

49175 PENA BLANCA SPRINGS — THE LONE STAR STATE'S MOST LEGENDARY METEORITE RECOVERY, CONTAINING ONE OF THE LARGEST EXTRATERRESTRIAL CRYSTALS EVER SEEN

Aubrite – AUB
Brewster County, Texas

In a widely known bit of meteorite Americana, it was on August 2, 1946 that several ranch hands were lounging near a stock pond in Brewster County, Texas, when a sonic boom pierced the tranquility. Minutes later the whistling sound of what seemed like an incoming mortar panicked the hands who, frozen by fear, next witnessed a large meteorite plunge in the pond directly in front of them. One of the hands dove in to recover the meteorite, and it was a good thing he did, because Pena Blanca is one of the very few meteorites that will dissolve in water. Pena Blanca is an aubrite, a very rare achondritic meteorite primarily composed of orthopyroxene enstatite. It is believed aubrites originate from asteroid 3103 Eger – a near-Earth orbiting asteroid whose spectrum matches perfectly with the aubrite subtype. There are only 67 aubrites known of the more than 40,000 meteorites known to exist, and more than half were found in Antarctica and are off limits to the collector. Now offered is a preeminent example of Pena Blanca. With a rim of fusion crust, and exhibiting the classic brecciation of aubrites, this specimen also features a giant crystal of enstatite – among the largest non-metallic, extraterrestrial crystals known to exist. Worthy of the finest natural history museums in the world, this is an outstanding specimen of a historic meteorite. 262 x 153 x 5 mm (10¼ x 6 x ¼ inches) and 892 grams (2.0 pounds).

Provenance: Macovich Collection of Meteorites

Estimate: $30,000-$42,500

49176 NWA 5974 — A LARGE COMPLETE SLICE OF A SUBLIME STONE METEORITE

L6

The Sahara Desert, near the Moroccan/Algerian Border

This is a beautiful complete slice from one of the larger stone meteorites found in the Sahara. Its ebony matrix provides a dramatic contrast to the galaxy of nickel-iron grains which are suspended throughout. This complete slice is rimmed in fusion crust-the result of meteorite's blazing descent through the atmosphere. Meteorites are named after the locality to which they are "delivered" so that researchers can speak of a specific meteorite without any confusion as to the meteorite referenced. Thus, meteorites are named after rivers, streams, mountains, cities, counties or basically any geological feature or marker of civilization which allows the specimen to be distinguished. In the Sahara Desert where there are frequently few such markers, geological or otherwise, the Nomenclature Committee of the Meteoritical Society decided to number the meteorites found in what they designated as the North West Africa (NWA) corridor encompassing much of the Sahara. Thus, NWA 5974 is the 5974th meteorite to be classified that was recovered from this region, and this is an exquisite specimen of an uncommonly pristine meteorite. 280 x 154 x 3 mm (11 x 6 x ⅛ inches) and 618 grams (1.3 pounds).
Estimate: $1,700-$2,200

49177 NWA 5717 — A PARTIAL SLICE OF AN EXTREMELY IMPORTANT NEW METEORITE, SUBTYPE 3.05, UNCHANGED SINCE ITS ORIGINS IN THE GASEOUS SOLAR NEBULA

CH-UNGR (Ungrouped Chondrite) Subtype 3.05

Western Sahara

Of the tens of thousands of *chondritic* meteorites known to exist (meteorites which contain silica-rich spherules, which is to say most meteorites), there are just 14 which are unclassifiable and have been designated as being ungrouped (CH-UNGR). NWA 5717 is the only meteorite within this select group (and one of the only meteorites, period) which also features a 3.05 subtype, making it among the most primitive planetary matter known. Unlike 99.99% of all other meteorites, NWA 5717 is unchanged since its origins in the early solar nebula. NWA 5717 originates from a previously unknown parent body (making it unique) and entirely separately, it also happens to be an example of the most primitive planetary matter ever before encountered. Only six pounds of similarly primitive material was known to exist prior to NWA 5717's discovery. States researcher Dr. Anthony Irving of Washington University, "There will most certainly be a great deal of research done on 5717 in years to come." Devoutly sought-after by scientists, unmetamorphosed meteorites like NWA 5717 represent the raw ingredients from which our solar system formed. Accordingly, more than half of the NWA 5717 mass will be placed in institutions and very little material will be available to the collecting community. Containing two lithologies and loaded with chondrules, this is a fine partial slice of a meteorite from which other specimens will soon be in most major collections. Accompanied by the 2010 Lunar and Planetary Science Conference abstract, *"The Extra-Ordinary Chondrite: NWA 5717."* 43 x 30 x 2 mm (1¾ x 1 x 1⁄16 inches) and 9.114 grams.
Estimate: $1,000-$1,600

49178   A SLICE OF THE TUCSON RING — THE MOST UNIQUE IRON METEORITE IN THE WORLD

Iron, anomalous, structural ataxite

Box Canyon, Near Tucson, Arizona

The Tucson Ring is the most well known iron meteorite in the world primarily because of its exotic shape but also because of its storied history. It was first reported by Jose Velasco of Sonora, Mexico in 1845 from his treatise on mining in the region. He described a mountain pass, Puerta de los Muchacos (today known as Box Canyon), in the Sierra de la Madera range (Santa Rita Mountains today) where large masses of pure iron were found at the base of the mountains. He described how one of the medium-sized masses was taken to Tucson, 30 hard miles away, where it was used as an anvil for the garrison blacksmith. Somehow a second large mass was taken to the garrison between 1845 and 1850 again to be used as an anvil, and this meteorite became known as "The Carleton". Pieces of the Ring were analyzed in 1852 and determined to be of meteoritic origin. In 1856, The Ring was retired from service as an anvil and moved. In 1860, a medical officer Bernard Irwin located the abandoned Ring and took possession of it for the Smithsonian Institution. The Carleton went west to California for display until 1939 when it was purchased by the Smithsonian and reunited with the Ring in Washington.

The Tucson Ring is unusual in that its mineralogy indicates that it was formed during a cataclysmic event whereby a small planet or asteroid was blasted apart by gravitational shear or impact with another body. As the body broke apart, the molten material ejected into space cooled and formed meteoroids and possibly smaller asteroids. The Tucson Ring cooled very quickly, indicating that it was part of a smaller remnant mass from the core or mantle of the destroyed planetoid. This is proven by the fact that the nickel-iron did not have time to crystallize and form the distinctive Widmanstatten figures that characterize and identify most iron meteorites. The Tucson Ring will not show Widmanstatten figures when etched because it was quenched quickly after the cataclysm. The Ring also has inclusions of clear glasses, further proving that it was quickly cooled. The Tucson Ring is the most highly sought-after iron meteorite in the world because only a small piece was removed from a knob on the inside margin of the Ring for analysis by the Smithsonian and no more will ever be removed. This means that the supply of this meteorite amounts to only a few hundred grams available to all of the scientific institutions and collectors worldwide.

An excellent part slice of this exotic and extremely rare meteorite weighing 4.7 grams and measuring 25 x 15 x 2 mm thick (1 x ½ inches) and showing some of the small glass silicate inclusions that characterize this famous meteorite.

Estimate: $2,400-$3,000

49179   IMILAC — THE INTERIOR AND EXTERIOR OF A METEORITE WITH SPACE GEMS REVEALED

PAL – Pallasite

Atacama Desert, Chile

Less than 1% of all meteorites are *pallasites*, the most sought-after of all meteorites. The dazzling, rarely available, end piece now offered amply reveals why Imilac is among the most coveted. The "pallasite" designation is in honor of the German scientist Peter Pallas, who discovered the first pallasitic mass in 1749 in Siberia. This is an honor Pallas is fortunate to have received, for he fervently believed that the unusual specimen he found could not be from outer space. Well, it was...and so is the wondrous meteorite from which this end piece is derived. Pallasitic meteorites originate from the mantle-core boundary of a planetary-sized body that broke apart during the formation of our solar system – the remnants of which are the *asteroid belt* between Mars and Jupiter. The olivine crystals seen here are the result of small chunks of stony mantle becoming suspended in molten nickel-iron and slowly cooling and crystallizing over a million years in the vacuum of outer space. The gleaming cut surface reveals a wealth of crystallized olivine as well as *peridot* (birthstone of August). The reverse, exterior surface of the meteorite is swathed in a milk chocolate patina. End cuts are obviously difficult to obtain, and this example provides a superb display of both the interior and exterior surface of an exotic meteorite. Recovered from the Atacama Desert in Chile, the highest desert on Earth, and with a Macovich Collection provenance, the finest collection of aesthetic meteorites in the world. 151 x 77 x 39 mm (6 x 3 x 1½ inches) and 445 grams (1 pound).

Estimate: $6,500-$8,000

49180   IMILAC — COMPLETE SLICE OF A METEORITE WITH SPACE GEMS

PAL – Pallasite

Atacama Desert, Chile

Similar to the previous lot, pallasites are the most sought-after meteorites, and this dazzling complete slice amply reveals why. Containing a spectacular mosaic of olivine and peridot crystals suspended in its polished nickel-iron matrix, this is a select complete slice of a pallasite with a full rim of fusion crust. Found in the Atacama Desert in Chile, the highest desert on Earth, the source material has been thoroughly excavated, and it has become more difficult to obtain complete slices of what is inarguably some the most resplendent extraterrestrial material known to exist. 168 x 99 x 3 mm (6½ x 4⅛ inches) and 145 grams (⅓ pound).

Provenance: Macovich Collection

Estimate: $3,500-$4,500

49181 LIBYAN DESERT GLASS — WHEN AN ASTEROID AND THE EARTH COLLIDE

The Sahara Desert at the Libyan/Egyptian border

The present offering is among the finest large-sized Libyan Desert Glass specimens known. Worthy of the finest natural history museums, it's extremely rare for large specimens to be as translucent, with as much saturation and as few blemishes as the example now offered. Libyan Desert Glass has been revered by early Egyptian civilization and found in Egyptian tombs. Its origin was long considered a mystery, but scientists now agree it is the result of an asteroid slamming into Earth 28.5 million years ago. Meteorite components have been found embedded in Libyan Desert Glass. The extraordinary heat and pressure that resulted from this impact liquefied terrestrial rocks and sand, which was splashed into the upper atmosphere before returning to Earth as solidified glass. This specimen was found in an extremely remote area of the Sahara Desert referred to as the Great Sand Sea, an area so remote and inhospitable that when a scientific team went to explore the locality, a previously missing Egyptian plane was discovered, intact, with the remains of its passengers who had died of thirst. The muted yet lustrous surface appears to have been sandblasted, and that is precisely what occurred over millions of years of natural sandblasting by desert winds. Accented further by elongated ribbing and a hint of scalloping, this natural glass sculpture is a matchless example originating from what would today be a worldwide catastrophic event – a massive asteroid impact. 154 x 151 x 109 mm (6 x 6 x 4¼ inches) and 1998 grams (4.4 pounds).

Estimate: $4,250-$5,500

49182 LIBYAN DESERT GLASS

Libyan/Egyptian border
Sahara Desert

Similar to the previous lot, but smaller. Tektites are silicated glass formations whose origin was long considered a mystery. Today scientists agree this phenomenon, whose name comes from the Greek *tektos*, meaning "melted," is the result of an asteroid slamming into Earth. The extraordinary heat and pressure that result from such impacts liquefy terrestrial rocks, which are splashed into the upper atmosphere before returning to Earth as solidified glass. This is a select translucent example of the smooth, golden tektites found in the sands of the Sahara Desert between Libya and Egypt featuring a translucency, scalloping and sandblasting of the very best examples. 69 x 59 x 41 mm (2¾ x 2¼ x 1½ inches) and 135.4 grams.

Estimate: $350-$450

49183 MOLDAVITE TEKTITE — METEORITE GLASS

Moldau River Valley, Czech Republic

Moldavite is a variety of Tektite named for the river valley in the Czech Republic where it was first found, the result of an asteroid impact that created the 14.5 mile diameter Nördlinger-Reis crater near Stuttgart in Germany almost 15 million years ago. Moldavite is prized for its clarity, shape and lovely green color; it was valued as a talismanic object in Paleolithic times, worn as pendants in the Middle Ages, and in the 17th to 19th centuries it was often offered by men to their fiancées as a charm to assure harmony in their forthcoming marital relations. This is a fine example, with a beautiful deep green color and translucent edges and a characteristically pitted bloom-like texture, 2¼ x 1¼ x ¾ inches and weighing 1.05 oz (29.8 grams).

Estimate: $350-$500

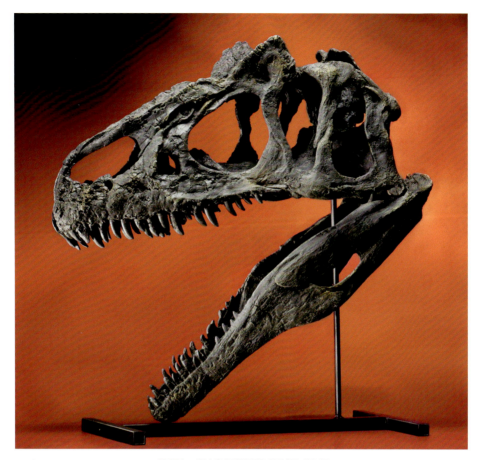

49184   ALLOSAURUS SKULL CAST
Allosaurus jimmadsoni
Jurassic
Morrison formation, Dana Quarry, Washakie County, Wyoming

The Allosaurus was a large fierce theropod dinosaur, the T-Rex of the Jurassic, 150 million years ago. It grew up to 30 feet in length and was armed with a mouth full of knife-like teeth. This is the first cast of the recently excavated Allosaurus skull from the Dana Quarry in Wyoming; This particular Allosaur was named "Dracula" because it was discovered with almost all of its teeth in place, an almost unheard-of characteristic; usually, if present, the teeth have fallen from the jaw bone, but this was a rare instance of the complete dentary arrangement being preserved. Of all the Allosaur fossils discovered, "Dracula" represents one of the very few with a fully articulated, undistorted skull. Most Allosaurs are found with their skulls in fragments and loose piles; but "Dracula" was articulated, allowing a rare look for researchers into the exact position and orientation of Allosaur skull bones. This cast skull is a faultless reproduction of an exceptional fossil, showing off its superlative bone texture and unique dentition, measuring 29¾ inches long, 30¼ inches high on a custom metal display stand.
Estimate: $1,800-$2,200

49185 FINE SABER-TOOTHED CAT SKULL CAST

Smilodon fatalis
Pleistocene
Rancho La Brea Formation, Los Angeles, California

Official State Fossil of California, the Great Saber-toothed *Smilodon fatalis* is the epitome of the North American fossil. It roamed across the entire New World throughout the last Ice Age 1.8 million to 10,000 years ago, but their remains are found nowhere else outside of the Americas. A member of the family of true cats (*Felidae*) its most striking and unique features are found in the skull and teeth, instantly recognizable from the giant curving upper canines that provide its name. It is presumed that these fangs were used to immobilize prey that might have been much larger and stronger than the cat itself. Saber-toothed cat fossils are highly prized, the most desirable being those excavated from the La Brea Tar Formation in California, but their immense rarity and frequently inferior condition and incompleteness make them an impossible dream for most collectors. A fine substitute is this exquisitely executed cast, finished with the lovely dark brown woody patina characteristic of tar-buried fossils, and boasting lovely ivory-colored teeth with 7½-inch long sabers, 12½ inches high overall on a custom metal display stand.
Estimate: $800-$1,200

49186 THE "DINOSAUR BIRD" — ARCHAEOPTERYX CAST

Archaeopteryx lithographica
Late Jurassic
Solnhofen formation, Eichstätt, Germany

This cast was taken from one of the most important fossils ever discovered, the Berlin Archaeopteryx. Discovered in 1876 or 1877 (and initially bartered in exchange for a cow!) It was the second specimen of this remarkable creature discovered, the most complete and the first with a complete head. The significance of the Archaeopteryx lies in its being a "missing link" between the theropod dinosaurs and today's birds; recognizably bird-like in form with extensive primitive feathers, the oldest such known, its osteology is in fact much closer to that of the dinosaurs and, first discovered in 1861 only two years after the publication of Darwin's *On The Origin of Species*, it has always held a key place in debates over evolution. Portions of only 11 examples have ever been discovered, the first being a sole feather. The specimen in the Humboldt Museum für Naturkunde in Berlin is especially important as it has been the subject of the most research into the bird's feathers. Here they are spectacularly displayed, with two full wings widespread, a long lizard-like tail with extensive plumage, and curious "trouser" feathers of a downy nature along its legs. The three-dimensionality and detail on this already extraordinary specimen is outstanding, from the tiny blood grooves on its curving claws to the row of tiny dinosaur-like teeth. A spectacular reproduction of one of the most significant fossils in the world, it has been meticulously cast and hand-painted, presented on a matrix 19 x 15¾ inches.
Estimate: $350-$500

49187   MATING MIDGES IN AMBER
Eocene
Samland Peninsular, Russia

Amber-entrapped insects are rare but rarer still are those preserved in copula, as here. This remarkable snapshot of the life cycle of the prehistoric midge comes from the famous amber deposits of the Baltic region of north-western Russia. The pair of tiny insects were going about their natural business when a slow inexorable ooze of tree resin overcame them. Over 40 million years later, they remain perfectly preserved as though in suspended animation, locked together in a ghastly mating ritual for all eternity. Every last detail of their anatomy and reproductive activity can be observed through the pale golden amber nugget, polished into a lovely little cabochon and exhibiting remarkable clarity with no other significant inclusions, approximately 1 x ⅝ x ¼ inches.

Estimate: $800-$1,200

49188   RARE FEMALE MOSQUITO IN AMBER
Culicidae family
Oligocene
La Toca Mines, Dominican Republic

The marvelous amber deposits of the Dominican Republic are a window into the neo-tropical ecosystem of this area 30-40 million years ago. The sticky resin of the Hymenaea protera tree has hardened into beautiful golden amber and, on rare occasions, any plant or animal life caught in the ooze is preserved forever in suspended animation. This elongated nugget is just such a window back in time, containing an unfortunate mosquito that indicates the presence both of standing water and of warm-blooded vertebrates in the Oligocene forests of the region. With fine clarity, the nugget allows a matchless view of the insect's anatomy; a female, it displays folded wings, long delicate legs, feathered antennae and a prominent proboscis. Of elongated form and polished, this superb specimen measures 1½ x ¾ x ½ inches.

Estimate: $600-$800

49189   FLY IN AMBER
Diptera Order
Oligocene
Dominican Republic

This is a large and beautifully colored amber nugget of exceptional clarity, a gilded cage for the unfortunate fly that was engulfed by oozing tree resin 30 million years ago. It is preserved in immaculate detail, exactly as in life, with every aspect of its tiny anatomy perfectly visible in the pale yellow polished cabochon, 1⅜ x 1⅜ x ⅝ inches.

Estimate: $350-$500

49190   THREE FLYING ANTS IN AMBER
Hymenoptera Order
Oligocene
Dominican Republic

Amber has been prized since at least Neolithic times for its delicate golden beauty, but among collectors the most sought-after specimens are those that contain once-living creatures caught in the sticky ooze of 30 million year-old tree resin. This is a great example, containing no less than three flying ants, perfectly preserved down to the tiniest detail of their delicate wings in a lovely soft yellow polished amber cabochon, 1 x ¾ x ½ inches.

Estimate: $350-$500

49191   FLY AND MAYFLY IN AMBER
Diptera and Ephemeroptera Order
Oligocene
Dominican Republic

One of the wonders of the prehistoric world is fossilized tree resin from the neo-tropical *Hymenaea protera* in what is today the Dominican Republic. Amber from this region is renowned both for its clarity and for its remarkable insect inclusions, as perfectly demonstrated by the present specimen. This lovely little nugget contains not one but two perfectly preserved insects, a fly and a mayfly, their tiny delicate anatomy completely visible within the golden yellow polished cabochon, 1 x ⅞ x ½ inches.
Estimate: $350-$500

49192   AMBER-ENTRAPPED ROACH
Blattaria Order
Oligocene
Dominican Republic

30 million years ago in the lush neo-tropical forests of today's Dominican Republic, the slow ooze of tree resin creeping down the trunk of a Hymenaea protera tree caught this roach unawares and preserved it forever in a beautiful golden prison. This is a large example of the rare faunal inclusions found in amber, ½ inch long, with the roach's prehistoric anatomy perfectly visible, from the slender transparent veined wings to the hairy spindly legs. Containing various other tiny insects the nugget has been polished into a beautiful soft yellow cabochon 1⅛ x 1 x ¼ inches.
Estimate: $600-$800

49193   SUPERB SCORPION AND MITE IN AMBER
Scorpiones and *Acariformes*
Oligocene
La Bucera Mine, Dominican Republic

This spectacular nugget shows just why the Dominican Republic is famed for its amber deposits, and for the rare instances of insect and animal inclusions. Sticky tree resin hardens over millions of years to become the lovely golden amber, and any creature trapped in the ooze is imprisoned for all eternity. Such instances are rare and most are mites or other tiny bugs; the present nugget contains an excellent Velvet Mite, perfectly visible down to the tiny body hairs. But the real point of interest in this specimen is an extremely rare, large and spectacular scorpion. The well-preserved scorpion is clearly visible and poised in attack mood with extended claws and curled metasoma (tail) terminating in a wicked-looking telson (barb). Also perfectly visible are the creature's pectine combs, V-shaped sense organs and chemoreceptors on the underside of the body unique to the scorpion, with which it sweeps the ground for texture and suitability for depositing spermatophore during the reproductive process. With various pieces of floral debris, the nugget has been polished into an oval cabochon and measures 1⅜ x ⅞ x ½ inches – a truly world-class specimen.
Estimate: $14,000-$18,000

49194   TRIO OF INSECT-BEARING AMBER NUGGETS
Eocene
Samland Peninsular, Russia

This Lot represents a fascinating glimpse into the insect life of the 50 million year old forests of the Baltic region of northwestern Russia; resin from the Sciadopitys conifer dribbled slowly down the trunk, capturing these unsuspecting mites in its inexorable path, preserving them for all eternity each in a lovely clear golden prison. Of the three specimens, the largest contains a tiny fungus gnat and has been polished into an oblong cabochon approximately 1½ x ⅝ x ⅜ inches; a slightly larger gall gnat is encased in a triangular cut piece approximately ¹³⁄₁₆ x ⁹⁄₁₆ x ¼ inches; and another fungus gnat is encased in the third piece, cut into a rectangular slab with two holes drilled through suggesting that the piece was once used as jewelry, approximately 1¼ x ½ x ⅛ inches.
Estimate: $200-$300

49195 LARGE AMBER NUGGET WITH LARGE LEAF AND NUMEROUS INSECTS

La Bucara Mine, la Cordillera Septentrional, Dominican Republic
A large Hymenaea leaf is the cornerstone of this large piece of Amber – well preserved with exquisite detailing, the leaf is accompanied by fungus gnats, a moth, midges, tiny larvae, gall gnats, a beetle, and a geometrid inch worm. This unusual specimen comes from a private Eastern collection and has been vetted by famed Amber expert Dr. David Grimaldi of the American Museum of Natural History. It measures 3⅛ x 3¼ inches.
Estimate: $2,500-$3,500

49196 ACACIA FROND CAPTURED IN AMBER

La Bucara Mine, la Cordillera Septentrional, Dominican Republic
A sizable section of an Acacia frond has been captured for eternity in this piece of Dominican Amber and is accompanied by a large winged male ant that appears to be strolling on the frond itself. Looking like its modern day cousin, the frond's individual leaves are well detailed. The Amber itself measures 1 x ⅞ x ⅜ inch thick and has been authenticated by famed Amber expert Dr. David Grimaldi of the American Museum of Natural History. From a private Eastern collection, it is in fine condition.
Estimate: $750-$1,000

49197 AMBER WITH RARE FLOWER PETAL AND INSECTS

La Bucara Mine, la Cordillera Septentrional, Dominican Republic
A delicately veined Hymenaea protera petal has been captured with all of its detailing in this piece of Dominican Amber that has been polished to reveal it and its accompanying menagerie of insects: salticid spider, worker ants, fungus gnat, psycodid flies, and ceratopogonid midge. Additionally there are resin pockets and bark debris. The Amber itself measures 1¾ x 1⅞ x ½ inches thick and has been authenticated by famed Amber expert Dr. David Grimaldi of the American Museum of Natural History. From a private Eastern collection, it is in excellent condition.
Estimate: $250-$350

49198 FINE AMBER CARVING

Oligocene
Dominican Republic
This is an exceptionally clear example of 30 million year old fossilized tree resin, beautiful honey-golden amber. As the resin seeps down the trunk of the tree it captures anything in its path, preserving the floral (and occasionally faunal) detritus forever. It is a rare piece that has no such inclusions, but a skilled artisan has capitalized on the remarkable and complete clarity of this piece to create a beautiful piece of natural history art; first cut and polished into a large cabochon, the amber has been flattened at the back, inset with numerous tiny leaves, and then reverse carved so that from the front one is presented with the tranquil scene of a deer grazing peacefully beneath a tree, with leaves further used to create two small birds flying by. A fine and unusual piece, it measures 3⅛ x 2 x ¾ inches.
Estimate: $1,600-$2,000

49199   RARE PARTIAL FOSSIL PALM FROND WITH FISH

Sabalites sp., Phareodus testis

Eocene

Green River Formation, Wyoming

This fossil palm frond plaque epitomizes the aesthetic beauty, the first-class preservation and the remarkable biodiversity of fossils found Green River Formation of Wyoming. Famed for its fish fossils, the area is also notable for its flora, soft material that in most other parts of the world decomposed before having a chance to be preserved in the fossil record. Palms are exceptionally scarce even here, however, as their thin leaves usually disintegrate and even if preserved, are easily lost amidst the sedimentary layers, and as a result they are highly prized by collectors. This dramatic plaque displays a large and fine example, and in a wonderful representation of Eocene life (50 million years ago) it is coupled for all eternity with an excellent inset specimen of the comparatively rare *Phareodus testis*, a fatter and less common fish than its sister the *P.encaustus*. This species is immediately identifiable from its long splayed pectoral fin and numerous sharp little teeth – the name means "to have tooth" – and even by the high standards of the Fossil Butte this is an excellently preserved example with superb detail and definition, of a good size at 12½ inches long. A world class plate, the fossils exhibits a lovely soft brown shading that harmonizes perfectly with the pale cream of the irregularly shaped 41 x 41-inch matrix.

Palm leaves are exceptionally rare and prized among collectors for being amongst the largest leaves in the fossil record. Palm leaves are very thin and usually degrade before fossilization can begin; it is only when a leaf is buried quickly and under the right conditions that it can be preserved. Several fossil fishes "swimming" on this plate add appeal to this 55 Million year old aquatic scene. This incredible plaque has been skillfully prepared by hand and comes with built-in hardware for easy wall hanging.

Estimate: $3,500-$4,500

49201 FOSSIL ROSE LEAF
Family Rosaceae
Eocene
Green River Formation, Wyoming
The Green River Formation provides a rare look into the flora and fauna of Wyoming, Colorado, and Utah from over 35 million years ago. Many ancestors of today's plants can be found as well preserved fossils in the ancient lake basins throughout the region. This fine specimen with excellent venation is a leaf from the Rosaceae family; possibly an ancestor of today's rose species. The leaf measures 5½ x 4 inches and is well centered on a limestone matrix measuring 13 x 9½ inches.
Estimate: $400-$550

49200 FINE FOSSIL SYCAMORE LEAF
Platanus wyomingensis
Eocene
Green River Formation, Wyoming
Well preserved plant foliage material in the fossil record is rare, due to the swiftness of decay and the generally delicate nature of leaves. From the important and famous fossil beds of the Green River formation, however, comes this wonderfully preserved sycamore leaf. The leaf has preserved venation leading from the stem and fine serrations along the margins. This fine specimen, measuring 7½ x 5½ inches, is a carbonized brown color in contrast to the gray matrix, measuring 11½ x 10 inches.
Estimate: $400-$550

49202 FOSSIL POPLAR LEAF
Populus wilmattae
Eocene
Green River Formation, Wyoming
Many fossil leaves of the Green River Formation have been identified by comparing their shape and venation patterns to those of modern leaves. These fossils are immensely important to science because they help map out the ancient floral family tree. This fossil poplar leaf, with excellent detail and venation, is very similar to the leaves of modern poplar trees. The specimen measures 4 x 2 inches and sits on a limestone matrix that measures 8¾ x 9½ inches.
Estimate: $150-$200

49203   FOLDED FOSSIL LEAF
Family Philodendron
Eocene
Green River Formation, Wyoming

Fossil foliage is difficult to preserve due to the delicate nature of leaves and the fact that they tend to decay quickly. This specimen demonstrates just how delicate plant material tends to be; this fossil leaf is likely from the Philodendron family and ripped along the mid-rib from the apex and folded over before it was buried and fossilized. The leaf is so well preserved that individual fibers can be seen throughout parts of the specimen and the folds of the leaf are obvious. The fossil leaf measures 9½ x 6 inches and rests on a matrix measuring 15 x 11 inches.
Estimate: $500-$600

49204   RARE PETRIFIED OAK SLICE
Quercus sp.
Miocene
Deschutes River, Oregon

Petrification of wood occurs over millions of years as silica-rich water infused with iron, manganese and other minerals seeps into the not-yet rotted trunks of trees and gradually replaces the original organic material on a cellular level; the wood turns to stone but retains its original structure and appearance in all but color. In some instances, one can even count the growth rings of the original tree, and such is the case with this lovely slab of ancient Oregon oak. Presenting a lovely soft palette of gray, cream and brown, the surface has been highly polished to a lustrous finish, but with the edge retaining its original rough bark texture. A less common specimen than the famed Arizona "rainbow" wood, it measures 18¾ x 16 x ⅝ inches.
Estimate: $650-$850

49205   FINE PETRIFIED WOOD SLAB
Araucarioxylon arizonicum
Upper Triassic
Chinle formation, Arizona

The "rainbow" wood of the Chinle Formation in Arizona is famed worldwide for its incredible array of colors. A 225 million year old forest, the giant trunks of the ancient Monkey Puzzle tree have been transformed inexorably over time by mineral replacement on a cellular level, different minerals providing different colors and creating some of Nature's most incredible natural canvases. The present specimen is of particularly high quality; whereas the polished slabs often have a cloudy nebulous patterning of colors, we can see here the original tree's growth rings in striking definition. The predominant shades are a lovely strong blue-gray and a deep velvety indigo, offset by black, white and dramatic splashes of vivid red-orange. The surface of this complete slice has been brought to a lustrous polished finish and the edge retains the natural rough bark texture; a fine-sized example of these highly desirable specimens, it measures 34⅜ x 27 x 1¼ inches.

Estimate: $3,000-$4,000

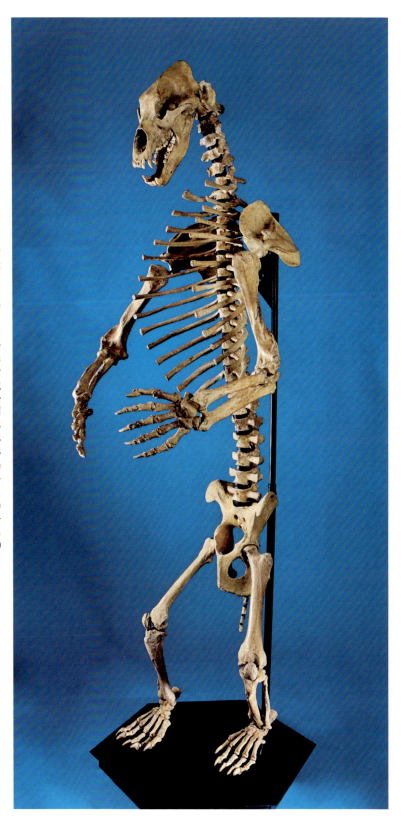

49206   FINE "CAVE BEAR" SKELETON

Ursus uralensis
Pleistocene
Russia

The extinct Siberian Bear was not in fact a true cave dweller like its cousin across the Urals in Romania and throughout Europe; skeletons of the two species are frequently confused, innocently or otherwise, but in practice are easily distinguished, most immediately by the distinctive crest shape atop the skull of the Siberian species. This is a superb example, expertly prepared and mounted, its arms outstretched in attack mode and its head cocked characterfully to one side as though contemplating its prey before tearing it to pieces with its huge vicious claws. These Ice Age bears were larger than any of their modern descendants and despite not being a true cave dweller, remains of the Siberian variety are found in large numbers in the caves in which they would congregate for hibernation. It is believed that their decline was due in part to hunting by early man; both the Neanderthals and Cro-Magnons are believed to have prized them as prey and prehistoric shrines utilizing the bears' skulls with evidence of spear-throwing suggest a semi-religious pre-hunt ritual. Of museum standard with superb bone texture, this monster (probably female) from the past stands an impressive 8 feet 4 inches high on a metal base, with an 18-inch long skull: a truly imposing addition to any collection.

Estimate: $24,000-$32,000

49207   MASSIVE SKULL OF AN EXTREMELY RARE EXTINCT CARNIVOROUS WARTHOG

Megachoerus zygomaticus

Upper Oligocene, 29 Million Years Old

Protoceras Sandstone, Shannon County, South Dakota

Warthogs are fearsome looking creatures that exist today in Africa. However, their huge sharp tusks and bony protuberances on their massive skulls are strictly defensive and used primarily to deter attack from the large carnivores prevalent on the African continent such as lions, leopards, crocodiles and hyenas, and less commonly when the males fight with each other during mating season. However, the lower tusks are also used for digging to find roots, fungi, small mammals and lizards that they often eat. Warthogs can reach up to 350 lbs and have been known to kill a lion through judicious use of their very sharp lower tusks. Roll back the clock 29 million years and we find quite a different animal indeed – this prehistoric monster weighed up to 2,000 lbs and grew to lengths of 11 feet or more. Their canines were more like giant crocodile teeth than tusks and measured up to five inches in length, roughly the size of the largest known T. rex tooth. They had huge jugal flanges, or cheek bones, to protect their massive jaw muscles from damage during battle, which resulted in their skulls being as wide as they are long. This animal, Megachoerus, was primarily a hunter and killer, preying on the abundant fauna of the late Oligocene, but was also omnivorous like the Bears of today. Megachoerus was faster than any Bear, however, and could probably run down the vast majority of its prey and quickly kill them with its massive canines. Indeed, almost nothing would be immune to attack from this behemoth since it was as large as the largest herbivores of its time. Imagine, if you will, a gigantic, nearly one ton, howling swine with five inch fangs chasing you at over 30 miles per hour – certainly there cannot have been many creatures in our planet's history more terrifying than these "killer pigs"!

This exceptional specimen measures 37 inches long by 37 inches wide by 27 inches high and has been completely prepped from all of its matrix. All of the molars and premolars in the upper and the lower are original except the lower right first premolar, which is cast. The upper and lower right canines, and some incisors are cast and a few other teeth have been restored, but the skull overall is approximately 85% original bone. It is one of the largest specimens known at 37 inches and is as big and massive as a large carnivorous dinosaur skull. This truly impressive, museum quality fossil skull comes complete on a custom display stand.

Estimate: $45,000-$55,000

DIRE WOLF

Canis dirus
Pleistocene, Ranchlabrean stage
Rancho La Brea Formation, Wilshire Hauser Pit, California

49208   **SUPERB DIRE WOLF SKULL**

One of the most famous fossil sites in the entire world is the Rancho La Brea Formation of Southern California, home to Los Angeles' La Brea Tar Pits. Of the abundance of specimens recovered from the tar, perhaps the most evocative is the skull of the Dire Wolf, numerous examples of which make up an incredible display at the George C. Page Museum located at the Rancho La Brea Tar Pits. Despite their preponderance in the locality, however, exceptionally few specimens are held in private hands, and exceptionally few approach the quality of the present example. Wolves were particularly susceptible to entrapment in this area as it was a classic predator-prey trap; during the last Ice Age, tar seeps occurred in several locations in southern California, covered by benign ponds of cool water that attracted thirsty animals. Large thirsty herbivores would come to drink and the unlucky ones that stepped into the water would be trapped in the sticky tar bottom and pulled slowly downwards. As they struggled furiously to free themselves, their cries of panic would attract opportunistic predators such as the Dire Wolf. In their eagerness, however, the wolves would themselves become mired in the tar, their presence in such numbers due to their pack-hunting methods.

The Dire Wolf was related to the Gray, or Timber, Wolf (*C.lupus*), somewhat larger at about 5 feet in length but with shorter, stockier legs. The two species co-existed in North America for around 100,000 years, but the Gray Wolf proved the more successful and there are no direct descendants of the Dire Wolf today; they probably became extinct concurrent with the appearance of man on our continent, early Paleo-Indians being the likely culprits in the disappearance of most late Pleistocene megafauna.

This particular specimen comes from the Wilshire Hauser Pit, a construction site in the early 1970's across the street from the original tar pits. Today there is virtually no legal way to collect in the tar seeps, so tar pit specimens such as this are almost irreplaceable. Large carnivore specimens are always sought-after and Dire Wolf fossils in particular are highly prized by collectors because there are almost none in private hands. This exceptional specimen was professionally prepared, is virtually complete with only one portion of the lower jaw composited from another specimen. It measures 12½ inches in length, 6¼ inches wide and comes mounted on a custom display.
An outstanding example of a famous fossil from an historic site.

Estimate: $18,000-$24,000

49209   PATHOLOGICAL GIANT SABER-TOOTHED CAT SKULL
Machairodus giganteus
Late Miocene
Gansu Dragon Bone Quarries, Central Asia

The Miocene savannahs of central Asia literally teemed with life, much like the Serengeti plains of modern Africa. There were massive migrating herds of gazelle, ancient elephants such as Mastodon and Platybelodon, rhinoceros, giraffe and antelope along with an incredible variety of other types of non-herd animals. Huge carnivores such as giant hyenas the size of a bull, monstrous powerful bear-dogs larger than Kodiak bears but which could run as fast as a modern lion, 1,500 pound carnivorous wart hogs, and giant saber-toothed cats all evolved to harvest this incredible bounty. The undisputed king of the Miocene and top carnivore of this savage time was the Machairodus giganteues, the largest saber-tooth cat of all time! With its huge serrated sabers and powerful muscles, this fearsome hunter was well equipped to bring down the all but the very largest prey.

This incredible specimen was saved from destruction in the late 1990's from the "dragon bone" miners who make their living digging up fossil bones and teeth which will be ground-up into to powders for use as traditional Chinese medicines. It is an outstanding specimen with only about 5% restoration and a complete set of nearly perfect teeth. This individual probably died from a massive infection after suffering grievous injuries in battle. The evidence can be seen in the row of healed perforation holes in the right zygomatic arch that range in diameter from 1 mm up to 13+ mm, the large penetration completely through skull at the back upper part of the braincase measuring almost 19 mm in diameter, a small 5 mm hole at the front of the right eye orbit, a larger 7 mm hole above the right saber, a large bone spur at the top of the left eye orbit, and a massive broken and healed area on the right side of the nose (right nasal bone). Based on the size of the perforations, the injuries were probably the result of a fight with a giant hyena. Since all of the perforations and breaks are healed around the edges, this cat lived for at least another 6 months after his mortal confrontation. Since the perforations did not close, we know that infection prevented bone growth to cover the holes as a result of continuous pus drainage from the affected areas. Pathological specimens such as this are very rare and highly prized by collectors. In addition, the atlas vertebrae remains attached to the occipital condyle at the back of the skull on this specimen which is very unusual. Both sabers are complete and retain the fine serrations that helped make them such effective and deadly weapons (much like a pair of steak knives) in jaws that could exert over 1,000 lbs of force. The bone is an attractive pinkish-cream color with reddish oxide and black dendrites. The teeth are of exceptional quality and are a beautiful lustrous yellow-cream color with black checking. This exceptional skull measures 14¼ inches long by 12¾ inches tall by 6¼ inches across the cheekbones or "zygomatic arches" with fearsome 4 inch sabers. It comes complete with a custom-made ebonized steel stand.

Estimate: $28,000-$35,000

49210 WOOLLY MAMMOTH TUSK

Mammuthus primigenius
Pleistocene
Siberia, Russia

A beautiful example of a highly collectible ice-age relic, this specimen displays a well-preserved root canal and the classic double curve of the mammoth tusk. It is colored with a gorgeous range of muted yellows and browns, the tonal shifts creating bands and striations along the whole of its length – 5 feet, 10½ inches along the outside curve. Although some damage to the surface near the tip has been restored, the missing sections of surface enamel reveal the darker ivory beneath, highly polished and with natural patterning that resembles nothing so much as the growth rings found in beautifully aged and darkened wood. Comes complete with a custom display stand.
Estimate: $8,500-$10,000

49211 FOSSIL PENILE BONE

Odobenus rosmarus
Alaska

The sexual organs of the human male are relatively unusual amongst mammals, in that they do not have a penile bone, or baculum. Theories as to this lack include an evolutionary aid to the reproductive females' selection process (insufficient blood pressure adequately to maintain an erection may indicate health problems such as diabetes, neurological disorders or even stress and depression – undesirable attributes in a potential mate); more whimsically, the bone is sometimes identified with the rib of Adam from which Eve was created (the Hebrew word translated as "rib" is far less specific than the English, and in addition that language has no word for "penis"). Most other mammals do possess this bone, however, and in the Inuit cultures of northern America and Greenland those of the walrus, seal and polar bear are frequently polished and used as clubs, handles for knives and other tools, as ritual objects. This is a fine example from a Northern Pacific Walrus, highly polished but retaining the honeycomb bone structure at either end, with an attractively creamy-gray mottled patina and measuring 19⅛ inches long.
Estimate: $300-$500

49212 FOSSIL DROPPINGS

Coprolite/Cololite
Miocene
Toledo, Washington

This superb specimen is from an abundant locality in Washington State and represents finds that have been the subject of some controversy. Coprolite is the name coined by renowned paleontologist William Buckland for fossilized excrement, and the present specimen certainly has the correct appearance. However, the absence of internal inclusions in these specimens and lack of associated vertebrate remains has prompted scholars to categorize them as ferruginous pseudofossils, natural concretions whose evocative form has misled overly-keen fossil hounds. More recently, scholarship has been tending toward the theory that these are indeed fecal in origin, but that they are actually intestinal casts (cololite), possibly from a species of sloth, and even judging by appearance alone, this is the most persuasive conclusion. With a brown and gray patina and crackled texture that really does suggests dried excrement. The present specimen is a fine example, and measures 7¾ inches long.
Estimate: $400-$500

49213 GIANT TRIASSIC REPTILE SKULL SECTION

Metoposaurus diagnostics kweichowensis
Late Triassic
Krasiejow, Poland

This curious-looking specimen is the rare skull plate from a Metoposaur, a giant salamander-like amphibian that lived at the end of the Triassic Period 200 million years ago. Despite its short, weak legs it was a predatory creature, using its cavernous mouth to scoop up fish and demolishing them with an array of fine sharp teeth. As an amphibian, it had lungs instead of gills and like the lung fish it could withstand seasonal water shortages by laying dormant in the exposed river mud; it is further notable for being one of the first amphibians to develop an otic notch, the membrane-covered opening that acts like an ear to detect airborne sounds (although recent scholarship disputes this function). Most Metoposaur skulls are found as small scattered fragments, but the present example comprises large sections most likely from the same individual with only 10-15% restoration. It is extremely well-preserved with highly textured bone quality and exhibits fine contrasting detail on both upper and lower surfaces. It displays little distortion and features well-defined eye and nasal sockets, and measures 14 x 11 inches. Comes complete with a custom metal display stand and oak base, 12⅝ inches high overall.
Estimate: $8,500-$10,000

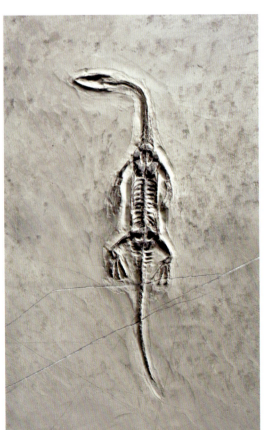

49214 AQUATIC REPTILE FOSSIL

Keichousaurus hui
Triassic
Tingziao Formation, Guizhou Province, People's Republic Of China

The Keichousaur is one of the most emblematic fossils of the abundant Triassic fossil deposits of central Asia. They were victims of the Triassic-Jurassic extinction event but as early aquatic reptiles, their physiognomy survived in the form of the Plesiosaur, Pliosaur and Elasmosaur, in whom the long slender feet evolved into more paddle-like extremities. In fact, these feet and the well-developed ulna in their lower arms suggest that it might have been amphibious, capable of subaerial locomotion. This is a well-detailed specimen, with good three-dimensionality, preserved in an attractive position with the long snaking neck, terminating in the distinctive arrow-shaped head. It measures 7 inches long as it lays and the good dark bone color stands in attractive contrast to the 11 x 7¾ inch gray stone matrix.
Estimate: $800-$1,200

49215   PERMIAN AMPHIBIAN AND FISH PLATE
Micromelerpeton, Apateon, Amplypterus, Paramblypterus
Permian, Rotliegendes series
Odernheim, Pfalz, Germany

The fossil beds of Pfalz in south-western Germany have yielded many marvelous Permian fossils, but today are long-closed to collectors, making such specimens increasingly rare on the market. The area is renowned for its fish and amphibian fossils, and the present natural assemblage is a perfect representation of the aquatic life that thrived in the area almost 300 million years ago. Over 35 individual specimens are present including two species of amphibians: the temnospondyl Micromelerpeton and the salamander-like Apateon, known also as the Branchiosaur, as well as two species of fish. Each is finely preserved with good detail and strong black coloring, leaping in pleasing aesthetic contrast from the swirling pale gray of the matrix. Fossils from this region are particularly difficult to extract and, as is a usual practice, the present plate was removed in sections and reconstructed on a fiberglass backing for stability. A wonderful portrait of ancient aquatic life, it measures 40⅝ x 28 inches.

Estimate: $8,500-$9,500

49216   SENSATIONAL FOSSIL FISH ASPIRATION
Mioplosus labracoides and Knightia eocena
Eocene
Green River Formation, Wyoming

The Eocene Fossil Lake Formation of Wyoming is the source of some of the finest fossil fish in the entire world, but even by its own high standards this specimen is exceptional. One of the predaceous perch-like Mioplosus met a sorry end as it tried to gobble down one of the lake system's populous herring-like Knightia, choking itself to death; 50 million years of fossilization has preserved the moment of its last meal as a snapshot in time forever. The detail to the fossils is superb, with excellent three-dimensionality to the larger fish's vertebrae and bony head, and the whole piece has been prepared to the highest standards. Fossil examples of one fish in the act of swallowing another (known as an Aspiration) are extremely rare, and few are as fine as this one; the Mioplosus measures 10⅞ inches long, the Knightia protruding a little over 2 inches from its mouth, and the dark brown of the fossils leaps dramatically from the pale limestone matrix 15¾ x 12½ inches.
Estimate: $2,800-$3,200

49217   FRAMED FOSSIL HERRING
Diplomystus dentatus
Eocene
Green River Formation, Wyoming, USA

There are some places where fossils are so well preserved, they look like pieces of art; the Green River Formation of Wyoming is one of fossil beds that produces such specimens. The Green River Formation is the sedimentary deposit from a series of giant inland lakes that covered the mountain states 40 million years ago. Diplomystus is an extinct freshwater fish that resembles today's herring and sardines and was quite prolific in the ancient lakes. The present specimen is excellently preserved with rigid bones that are expertly prepared with striking three-dimensionality in dark contrast to the surrounding tan limestone. The fossil fish measures 16 x 5 inches and the entire matrix is set in a lovely beveled wood frame measuring 28 x 21½ inches.

Estimate: $1,100-$1,400

49218   FINE FOSSIL PERCH
Priscacara serrata
Eocene
Green River Formation, Wyoming

The Green River Formation is renowned as the source of some of the finest fish fossils to be found anywhere in the world, and this reputation is only enhanced by the world-class skill of those who prepare the specimens. Even among such exalted company, the present example is an outstanding specimen of one of the 19 genera of fish to be found in these prehistoric waters. The name Priscacara means "primitive head", and the genus was shaped rather like the modern-day perch. In rare cases such as this, the Priscacara was preserved with its protective dorsal spines flared out in defensive position, resulting in an esthetic display. The details on the bones are exceptional; minute elements from the tail fins to the tiny teeth are all present and perfectly preserved. The fish itself measures 9 inches long, on a limestone matrix measuring 16½ x 12¾ inches.

Estimate: $650-$800

49219   FOSSIL FISH TILE MURAL

Priscacara liops, Knightia eocaena, Knightia alta

Eocene

Green River Formation, Wyoming

This highly decorative mural is comprised of 31 tiles of Green River limestone, sixteen of which each contains a beautifully preserved fossil fish. The Green River Formation is famed for producing some of the very finest fish fossils in the world, in great abundance and variety, and their high quality is perfectly demonstrated here. Every one of the fossils displays the exceptional detail and definition one expects from this locality; four of them are the plump and characterful *P. liops*, an extinct species of perch and a highly popular fossil from the region, and the remaining fish are a mixture of the *K. eocaena* and the less-common, fat-bodied *K. alta*, amongst the most populace species in these ancient waters. The tiles are arranged in a stepped diamond shape and the whole piece measures 71⅞ x 48 inches overall; with the strong dark brown of the fish standing in lovely contrast to the soft cream limestone, it makes for a superb and eye-catching display piece.

Estimate: $10,000-$14,000

49220   AN EXTREMELY RARE FOSSIL FISH POSITIVE AND NEGATIVE — COELACANTH "THE LIVING FOSSIL"

Caridosuctor populosum

Carboniferous, Late Mississippian

Bear Gulch Limestone, Fergus co., Montana

Having existed for over 300 million years, the Coelacanth was presumed to have vanished from our planet along with the dinosaurs during the KT extinction event, 65 million years ago. Then one day in 1938, one of these "living fossils" was caught off the coast of Africa; incredible enough, but then a second species was discovered in Indonesia in the late '90s (making them officially a Lazarus taxon, a species vanished from the fossil record that reappears some time later). Predatory lobe-finned fish, they are part of the lineage of limbed fish that crawled onto land and became the ancestors of all terrestrial animals. It is incredible that they have survived every major extinction event almost unchanged in the past 375 million years, but today they are considered an endangered species. This superb specimen was discovered in the 318 million year old Bear Gulch limestone of Montana, known for its amazingly well-preserved marine life, and the coelacanths represented there are rare but exceptionally detailed; the present example is among the best ever offered from the locale, so perfectly preserved that neither preparation nor touch-up was required. Not only that but, incredibly, it has been preserved in both positive and negative impressions, a highly rare occurrence in any case, and one especially difficult to excavate with success. The body is covered by a beautiful pattern of fine scales, the tassel-tipped tail is beautifully fanned out, and the skull exhibits exquisite bone structure. Finally, in a surfeit of exceptionalness, the specimen offered here is considered to represent a new genera and species of Coelacanth and is accompanied by copies of two academic articles on its classification. An absolutely world-class "living fossil" specimen in every way, the fish itself measures approximately 7¾ inches long in a limestone matrix approximately 15 x 10 inches.

Estimate: $6,500-$9,000

49221 DRAMATIC FISH-SKULL FOSSIL
Xiphactinus audax
Cretaceous, Santonian
Niobrara Chalk, Western Kansas, USA

This vicious-looking prehistoric bony fish roamed the warm shallow waters of the Niobraran Sea, or Western Interior Seaway, that split the continent of America in two halves for a large proportion of the Cretaceous period. A ferocious 20-foot long predator, it was second in the food chain only to the sharks, such as the Squalicorax, and to the monstrous Mososaur in these 85 million years old waters. The most famous example is a 15-footer with a complete 6-foot ichthyodectid Gillicus in its belly, to be found in the Sternberg Museum of Natural History, Hays, Kansas. First named in 1870 by Joseph Leidy, it remains still the object of a certain amount of nominal confusion, having been superfluously named the following year by E.D. Cope *Portheus molossus*. Although the Xiphactinus has no living relatives, it resembled a giant fanged tarpon and is known colloquially as the Bulldog fish; this dramatic specimen certainly conjures the strength and viciousness of its namesake, with the powerful jaws preserved in remarkable three-dimensionality, the left maxilla prepared entirely free from the matrix, bristling with frightful teeth (the longest measures 2 inches). In fact, these teeth were used primarily for securing its prey, as the Xiphactinus was in the habit of swallowing its meals whole, a dangerous practice that could result in severe damage to its internal anatomy as the smaller fish struggled in its death throes. The massive bony skull dominates the matrix, complete with the sclerotic ring that supported the eyeball, but also present is the pectoral fin, with fine three-dimensionality and texture throughout. With a strong dark brown coloring, the whole piece leaps vividly from the pale cream 52 x 34-inch irregular matrix, fully conjuring the aggressive and forceful nature of the fish.

Estimate: $18,000-$22,000

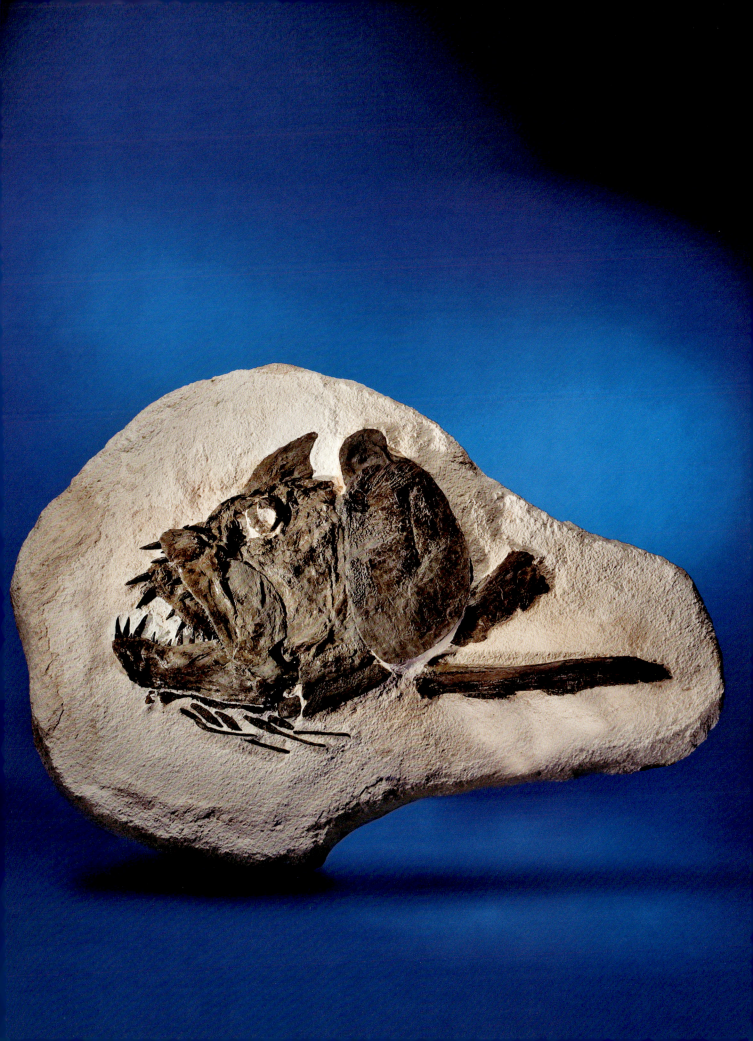

49222　LARGE MEGA-SHARK TOOTH
Carcharocles megalodon
Miocene
Ogeechee River, Georgia, USA

Picture a shark the size of a city bus, with a mouth big enough for a person to walk into, lined with several rows of these fearsome hand-sized teeth: that is the Megalodon, the greatest hunter of the planet's oceans who reigned supreme 15 million years ago. With a cartilaginous skeleton unpreserved by the fossil record, all that remains of this monster are its teeth, but what teeth they are – no wonder its name in Greek means "big tooth". Despite the hazardous conditions under which they must be recovered, in the cold murky depths of the sounds around the Carolinas and Virginias, they are highly sought-after by collectors. From a less usual location, this is a superb example with lovely mottled brown and gray patination, good enamel coverage and excellent serrations. It also boasts a particularly fat heavy root section and measures an impressive 5⅝ inches along the diagonal.

Estimate: $800-$1,000

49223　POLISHED MEGA-SHARK TOOTH
Carcharocles megalodon
Miocene
Ocean River, South Carolina

As big as a Greyhound bus, the fearsome Megalodon vastly outsized its nearest modern equivalent, the Great White Shark (*Carcharodon carcharias*). Based on the similarity of the ancient and modern teeth, the two species were long thought to be related, but a new genus (*Carcharocles*) introduced in 1995 relies on a theory of parallel evolution to explain the similarity, and posits the extinct broad-toothed Mako Shark (*Isurus hastalis*) as the Great White's likely ancestor. All that remains to us of this ancient monster today are its teeth, the cartilaginous skeleton having decomposed long before it could be preserved in the fossil record. It's no surprise that these teeth have become highly sought-after collector's items, and this is a particularly fine example. The polished enamel no longer quite retains its full coverage but more than makes up for that with terrific coloring: dark and pale gray streaked and patched with blue and highlighted by several gorgeous splashes of vivid orange. A fine large specimen, it measures 5½ inches along the diagonal.

Estimate: $800-$1,000

49224   RARE PRIMITIVE FOSSIL BIRD
Confuciusornis sanctus
Cretaceous, Aptian Stage
Yixian Formation, Sihetun Sites, Liaoning Province, China

Due to their delicate hollow bones, birds stand little chance of preservation in the fossil record; this specimen, however, is so fine that even the feather detail can easily be seen. Perfectly positioned, belly up and with its wings open, it is amongst the finest examples of its rare kind. The skull and primitive, edentulous beak are excellently preserved, and there is superb three-dimensionality to the limbs, right down to the curving raptor-like toe claws and the paired tail feathers that identify this specimen as a male. The first ancient bird to be discovered outside Germany, *Confuciusornis sanctus* retains many of the primitive dinosaurian features exhibited by the world famous Archaeopteryx specimens from Solnhofen, but has shed the bony tail vertebra in favor of a short, fused pygostyle bone, and is notable for its lack of teeth – the first recorded bird to exhibit these features. A tremendously important species, this 125 million-year-old bird is the earliest known beaked bird fossil and a fascinating link with the terrestrial dinosaurs. The fossil itself measures 10¼ inches long and is presented under Plexiglas in a mahogany frame, 18¾ x 13⅝ inches overall.

Estimate: $9,000-$12,000

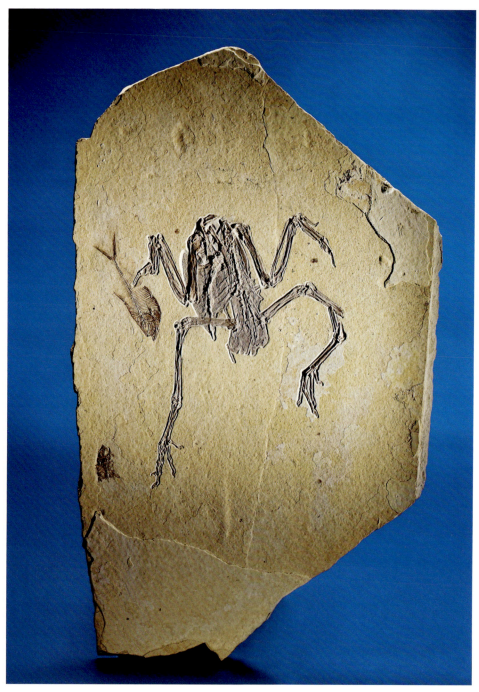

49225   SPECTACULAR FOSSIL BIRD
prob. *Gallinuloides wyomingensis*
Eocene
Green River Formation, Lincoln co., Wyoming

With their tiny, delicate, hollow bones, birds stand little chance of being preserved in the fossil record. The Fossil Butte in Wyoming, however, is famed for its ability to produce fossil after fossil of the most delicate and rarely-found fauna and flora, preserved in the most incredible detail and condition. The present specimen is superlative even by the standards of the area however: it is the spread-eagled body of a prehistoric galliform bird, first described in 1900, an ancestor of modern chickens, grouse, pheasant, quail and turkey. Somewhat unnervingly, it is lacking its head and long-ish neck, perhaps tucked beneath the body, but the remainder of the creature is preserved to perfection, right down to the tiny curved claws. The bones are all superbly well-defined, those of the arms and legs further exhibiting a remarkable three-dimensionality, bone texture and warm brown patination. The world-class quality of the fossil is only enhanced by its aesthetic positioning, as well as by the presence of a fat-bellied, 3⅛ inch long *Knightia eocena*, a common herring-like fish in the 50 million year old network of subtropical lakes of this region. The bird fossil itself measures 5⅛ inches wide by 7¾ inches long, in soft brown shades harmonizing attractively with the pale cream of the irregularly-shaped 17 x 10½-inch matrix.

Estimate: $18,000-$22,000

49226   FINE SHOVEL-NOSED TRILOBITE
Psychopyge termierorum
Devonian
Morocco

The trilobite is one of the strangest-looking creatures to be found in the fossil record, and the Psychopyge species is outstandingly bizarre even for this class. The long shovel-like rostrum protruding from the cephalon is immediately distinctive, used perhaps for scooping up food. The *P. termierorum* is considerably rarer than its cousin *P.elegans*, distinguished by an even longer snout and by the graduating axial spines. This is a superlative specimen, with finely-preserved compound eyes positioned high on the head and capable of 360° vision, useful to keep a wary eye out for predators, either side of a long freestanding hooked occipital spine. With the finest detail throughout, from the small pustules (bumps) at the front of the head to the long tapering genal (cheek) spines, this is a beautifully prepared specimen by Jeff Hammer, the finest trilobite preparitor in the World. With no restoration, this museum quality specimen measures 3½ inches long on a triangular matrix 3½ x 4⅞ inches.

Estimate: $5,000-$6,500

49227   EXCEPTIONAL TRILOBITE
Hollardops sp.
Devonian, Emsian stage
Timrhanrhart Formation, Jebel (Mount) Gara El Zquilma, Southern Morocco

Like a frozen moment in time this superlative specimen looks as if it were gliding down a gentle slope, pausing to raise its head and scan the surroundings with its 360° vision. The 390 million year old Hollardops is a classic archetypical trilobite, its neat form comprised of a slightly pointed cephalon (head) with trailing librigena and incredibly detailed faceted compound eyes; the distinctively ribbed thorax, compact and lined with short pleural spines; and the short spined phygium or tail. Of superb three-dimensional character obtained by Master Trilobite preparitor Jeff Hammer, this classic specimen measures 2⅜ inches along the curve of its body and displays a rich black coloring forming a terrific contrast with the pale limestone matrix, 2⅜ x 2¼ x 2¼ inches.

Estimate: $800-$1,000

49228 A WHISKERED SPINEY TRILOBITE

Kettneraspis sp.
Devonian, Emsian stage
Hamar Laghad Formation, Jebel (mount) Issomour, Morocco

This remarkable specimen presents a truly bizarre appearance. Bristling with spines of varying lengths, it also boasts exaggerated holochroal (compound) eye stalks and a long curved occipital spine. Its cephalon is even slightly raised from the matrix, offering a rare glimpse of the hypostome (mouth), gently curved to give it almost the appearance of a smile. Prepared to museum standard by Jeff Hammer it boasts incredible detail throughout, faultless three-dimensionality and lovely dark coloring which, unusually, shades almost to brown near the front of the specimen. Measuring 1⅜ inches long and 2⅛ inches between its long genal spines, it rests on a pale stone matrix containing a further fragment of a rather large specimen, 4½ x 4⅜ x 2½ inches overall.

Estimate: $2,500-$3,500

49229 FINE LONG-SPINED TRILOBITE

Cyphaspis sp.
Devonian
Hamar Laghdad formation, Achana , Morocco

With the exception of the fine stalk eyes, the entire head of this remarkable-looking trilobite is covered with bumpy pustules, so pronounced that some look almost like miniature spines. As for the actual spines, it boasts a long, tapering and impossibly delicate raised axial spine and a similarly slender pair of pustulose genal spines. Finely prepared by Jeff Hammer and relatively large for this genus, it measures 1⅜ inches long in a 3⅛ x 2¾ x 2-inch matrix.

Estimate: $1,500-$1,800

49230 FINE AND RARE TRILOBITE
Cyphaspis eberhardiei
Devonian, Emsian stage
Timrhanrhart formation, Jbel Gara el Zquilma, Southern Morocco
This rare trilobite comes from the 390 million year old Jbel Gara el Zquilma formation south of Foum Zquid in Morocco. Trilobites from this locality are exquisitely preserved and while several species are commercially available, their taxonomy has never been formalized. The jet-black exoskeleton of this typically excellent specimen contrasts beautifully with the light color of the matrix and emphasizes the long delicate genal and axial spines. Prepared by Jeff Hammer to museum standards, this specimen exhibits the finest detail, from the pustulose texture to the undulating ribbed surface of the thorax. Such small delicate creatures are incredibly difficult to extract from the ground and to prepare, making this a superlative example, 1⅛ inches long in a 2¼ x 2⅜ x 1⅜-inch matrix.
Estimate: $1,200-$1,500

49231 AN EXCEPTIONAL FOSSIL SEA SCORPION
Eurypterus remipes
Upper Silurian
Fiddler's Green Formation, Herkimer County, New York
Eurypterids, commonly called "Sea Scorpions," were the apex predators of the late Silurian Period 420 million years ago. The largest arthropods that ever lived, some species could grow to over 7 feet in length and were armed with sharp-toothed claws for ripping apart their prey and a tail (telson) that terminated in a fearsomely long spine. This is the source of their colloquial name but in fact they are more closely related to the horseshoe crab than to the scorpion, and subaerial trackways indicate that they were not exclusively marine in their habitat. Today, eurypterids are extremely rare in the fossil record and can only be found in a handful of locations worldwide: the best come from a small quarry in upstate New York, where typically one ton of rock may yield only one good specimen; their quality is such, however, that it holds pride of place as New York's State Fossil. This exceptional specimen comes from that very quarry and is amongst the top 1% of examples ever found in terms of both size and quality. Complete from the rounded head to the telson barb, with two paddle arms sticking out to the side, it exhibits a beautiful dark carbonized preservation in pleasing aesthetic contrast to the gray matrix, and no restoration. The specimen measures approximately 6¾ inches from head to tail and 6 inches across the paddles on a 8¼ x 6¼ inch matrix.
Estimate: $1,400-$1,800

49232   FINE PYRITIZED STARFISH

Furcaster paleozoicus
Devonian
Hunsrück slate, Bundenbach, Germany

The Hunsrück slate of southwestern Germany around Bundenbach is a rich fossil deposit famous for its exceptional fauna from the 400 million years-old Devonian Period, brilliantly preserved in metallic pyrite. Mined since ancient times for roof tiles and blackboards, the region has yielded over 260 species, mostly significantly arthropods and echinoderms, although other eumetazoa, mollusca and vertebrates have been recovered, and even the tracks of trilobites. The quality of the slate allows for preservation of the finest detail: the legs and antennae of arthropods and tube feet of echinoderms that would normally be lost remain beautifully preserved in the Hunsrück shales, assisted by the anoxic conditions that allow for pyritization. In fact, this quality makes the fossils easily identifiable under x-rays and many specimens from the region are first found by scanning large piece of slate in this fashion. The present superb specimen is of an oegophuroidea Furcaster, an extinct starfish ventrally preserved in its death pose in shimmering golden pyrite and extraordinary detail; gorgeous arms with tiny tubed feet, a star-shaped mouth, and excellent texture throughout its body are all perfectly visible. A typically first-class specimen from this region, it measures 3⅜ inches across on a trapezoidal dark slate matrix measuring 13 x 7⅞ inches.

Estimate: $750-$900

49233   LONG ARMED FOSSIL BRITTLE STARFISH

Ophiura graysonensis
Cretaceous
Dallas-Fort Worth region, Texas

The echinoderm Brittle Stars are closely related to starfish, with five slender whip-like arms and a central-mouthed body; they are distinct, however, in that rather than tubed feet, they use these arms as their mode of locomotion across the sea floor. The Brittle Star is still around today, surviving essentially unchanged for the past 500 million years, making it one of nature's longest-surviving success stories. The present specimen is of excellent quality and finely detailed, from the shallow but populous Cretacean sea of what is today the Dallas/Fort Worth region. The creature itself measures 3 inches across in a dark gray color that contrasts pleasingly with the paler gray of the 7¼ x 5⅜ x 1½ inch matrix.

Estimate: $500-$800

49234   PRECIOUS GEM AMMONITE
Placenticeras meeki
Cretaceous
Bearpaw Formation, Southern Alberta, Canada
A fine example of these highly sought-after specimens, this extremely bright and colorful ammonite flashes predominantly with fiery red on one side, whilst the other side is mostly a gorgeous golden green. This iridescent material is known as ammolite, one of the world's rarest precious stones and the result of millions of years of compression and the mineralization of iron, copper and silica precipitated from volcanic ash. The shimmering and ever-changing colors are caused by light refracting through and rebounding from thin platelets of aragonite, the primary constituent of the ammonite's nacreous shell lining. As with most specimens from the area, this one is significantly compressed, but retains good areas of three-dimensionality and is of good size, 17⅜ inches in diameter.
Estimate: $10,000-$16,000

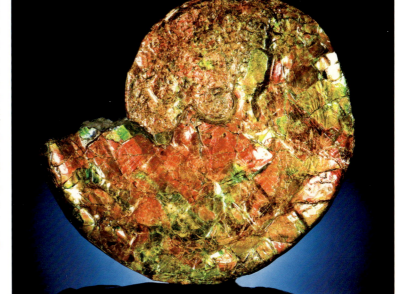

49235   IRIDESCENT GEM AMMONITE
Placenticeras meeki
Cretaceous
Bearpaw Formation, Southern Alberta, Canada
An exquisite example of precious gem ammolite, one of the world's rarest gemstones. The shell of this ammonite has been transformed over millions of years from plain old mother-of-pearl to the wonderfully colorful iridescent material we see today. This process is observed only in specimens from a small area of North America, making them among the most sought-after by fossil collectors. Most are subjected to intense compression, many emerging almost completely flat, but the present example retains a good degree of three-dimensionality, and flashes with lovely golden greens and reds, and even a hint of the much less common purple and electric blue. Of attractive size, it measures 11 inches in diameter.
Estimate: $8,500-$10,000

49236   SLICED PYRITIZED AMMONITE WITH CALCITE
Spitoiceras sp.
Volga River, Ulianovsk Area, Russia
Increasingly scarce on the market, these Russian ammonites are amongst the most unusual and fascinating of this abundant order of fossilized cephalopods. The present specimen is presented sliced in half with the inner faces highly polished to enhance the beautiful effect of pyrite-replacement; the outer (living) chambers of the shell have a mirror-like black metallic sheen with hints of a silvery lining, but this is one of the rarer specimens where the inner (buoyancy) chambers have been filled with lovely contrasting creamy yellow calcite. A highly attractive pair, they each measure approximately 9½ inches in diameter.
Estimate: $1,200-$1,600

49237   BRITISH AMMONITE

Arietites (Paracoroniceras) sp.
Jurassic, Lower Lias
Jurassic Coast, West Dorset, UK

This is a fine example of a classic British ammonite, its ribbed shell displaying the typical gentle contours and a lovely warm brown coloring. The Jurassic coast on the English Channel is a World Heritage site, famous for its abundant Jurassic fossil deposits (as well as treasures from both the Triassic and Cretaceous periods); houses and cottages throughout the area can be seen with ammonites of all sizes built into their brick and stone work, and even a casual stroller along one of the many beaches is likely to come across some relic of millions of years ago. One would be extremely lucky to stumble across an example of this size and quality, however; set in the original gray stone matrix it measures 13 inches in diameter.

Estimate: $2,600-$3,200

49238   VERY LARGE GEM SCAPHITE ON MATRIX

Jeletzkytes spedeni
Late Cretaceous

Fox Hills Formation, Cheyenne River, South Dakota

Scaphites are an extinct variety of cephalopod called ammonites which are related to the nautilus, squid and octopus of today. The modern nautilus retains its shell like the ancient ammonites, but the octopus and squid have either lost their ancestral shell completely or internalized it as a support structure like in squids. The Late Cretaceous seas of what is now the Great Plains of North America literally teemed with myriad varieties of these highly intelligent and very successful creatures, and that time period represented the pinnacle of their evolutionary diversity and abundance. Today all that remains of these ancient seas are the dark gray shale beds of the Fox Hills Formation on the slopes of the Black Hills and Rocky Mountains. The Fox Hills Formation produces the most diverse and beautiful specimens of fossil cephalopods in the world and are the mostly highly prized ammonites among collectors and scientists alike. The exceptional preservation of the Fox Hills Formation is on full display here as a rainbow of colors dances across this preserved scaphite shell, frozen in the dark gray matrix, with gorgeous "mother-of-pearl" iridescence in green, pink and silver. What makes this specimen exceptional, however, is its huge size – it measures over 5¹⁄₁₆ inches in diameter which places it amongst the largest know scaphite specimens. In addition, this specimen is an example of one of the most beautifully ornate species of scaphite, Jeletzkytes spedeni, known for its large parallel rows of "horns", deep latitudinal striations and very fat shell. This specimen measures 5¹⁄₁₆ inches in diameter by 1⅝ inches thick on a 6 x 6 inch matrix along with a baby Sphenodiscus ammonite and dozens of fossil clams and gastropods.

Estimate: $3,000-$3,500

GASTROPOD

Campanile giganteum
Eocene
Champagne, France

49239   GIANT FOSSIL GASTROPOD PAIR

The ancient Campanile is considered to be the largest gastropod that ever lived, reaching lengths of up to 2 feet. Its elegant tapering form and attractively textured and robustly contoured shell have made it a great favorite with fossil collectors. This is a particularly fine specimen boasting two good shells in an aesthetic pose. Like most French Eocene fossils, they boast a lovely clean chalky white color and are resting in an appropriately seashore-like limestone matrix, teeming with much smaller gastropods, bivalves and other marine life. One of the specimens has a 1-inch section of restoration at the tip and the larger of the two is almost entirely free from the matrix, of good size at 21 inches in length.
Estimate: $2,400-$3,000

49240   LARGE MASS MORTALITY ORTHOCERAS SLAB
Orthoceras sp.
Ordovician
Sahara Desert, near Talmud, Morocco

A study in black and white, this mass mortality plate of fossil cephalopods (Orthoceras sp.) shows that there were millions of these sea dwelling creatures in what was once the Sahara Seas (now known as the Sahara Desert). The individual specimens have been sculpted out of the matrix using hand tools and painstakingly polished, creating a three dimensional effect. Their shell remnants have all been oriented in the same direction by the rhythmic motions of the crashing waves, and fossilized over the eons. This dynamic fossil plaque shows the huge variation in size of these ancient relatives of the squid and chambered nautilus: some are a mere few inches long while the longest specimen is over two feet in length at 25½ inches. Overall dimensions are 55½ x 43 inches and it is approximately 5 inches thick. In fine condition.

Estimate: $1,800-$2,200

49241   FINE DOUBLE GEM AMMONITE WALL PLAQUE
Placenticeras meeki
Cretaceous
Bearpaw Formation, Southern Alberta, Canada
Gemstone ammolite is amongst the most sought-after of all materials in the world of fossil collecting, but its appeal is not limited
to those of a paleontological bent; as this beautiful twin ammonite display so amply demonstrates. The flashing colors of the
ancient ammonites' shells are highly decorative and were formed by millions of years of slow compression and mineral seepage
that has transformed the original nacrous lining into an iridescent canvas of red, orange and green, with hints of the rare blue and
purple. These two exceptionally fine specimens measure 10¼ and 6 inches in diameter and appear to leap from the subdued
dark shale matrix in dramatic contrast. The overall specimen measures 28 x 22 inches and is backed, ready for hanging.
Estimate: $20,000-$24,000

MOUNTED DINOSAUR

Jeholosaurus shangyuanensis
Lower Cretaceous
Yixian Formation, Central Asia

49242   EXCEPTIONAL NEW ORNITHOPOD DINOSAUR

First discovered less than ten years ago, the Jeholosaurus was a chicken-sized Ornithopod whose exact place in dinosaur taxonomy is still the subject of research. Its skeleton indicates immediately that it must have been a fast and agile runner, useful as its small size would have made it a delectable snack for the contemporary carnivorous therapods such as the dromeosaurids and early tyrannosaurids. It is suspected to be a close relative of the Heterodontosaurus whose name refers to the different types of teeth found in the jaw; the Jeholosaurus shares this characteristic, with flattened back teeth for masticating plant material and sharp and pointed premaxillary teeth at the front, more suited to a carnivorous diet. The overall suggestion is that Jeholosaurus was an omnivore, eating insects and possibly small lizards as well as plants. The present specimen is of exceptional quality, with over 80% original bone and virtually no distortion, more complete and of even better quality than the holotype. Excavated from the tuffaceous sandstone of the Yixian formation created by a massive volcanic eruption some 130 million years ago, it has lovely bone texture and patina; superbly prepared in a straight-spined, running pose with both forearms outstretched it measures 26 inches long and stands 11 inches high on an oak base. A superb specimen only enhanced by its rarity and absence from most museum collections.

Estimate: $24,000-$35,000

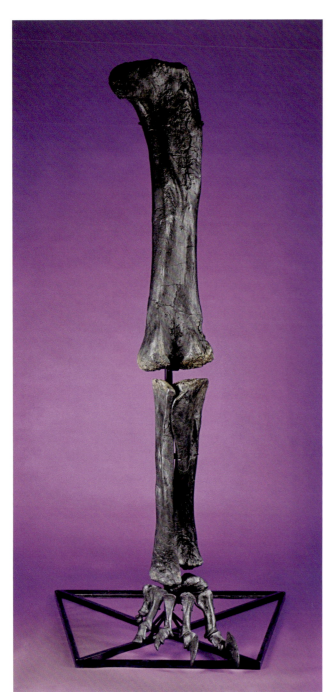

49243 LARGE DINOSAUR LEG
Diplodocus longus
Jurassic
Morrison formation, Dana Quarry, Washakie Co., Wyoming

The Diplodocus was one of the longest dinosaurs to ever roam the earth, often times reaching over 100 feet in length. It had a distinctive long neck and full body, and conforms to what many imagine as the "typical" dinosaur shape – huge beasts that were as big as a house. Numerous articulated dinosaur skeletons have been found recently in the Dana Quarry in Wyoming; the 150 million year old Jurassic sand and mudstone is thought to be an ancient watering hole where many dinosaurs, both predator and prey, met a grisly end trapped in the mud. This specimen from the quarry is an excellently articulated leg comprising twenty bones in their osteologically correct position, with superb texture and a gorgeous dark patination, mounted in a custom metal armature. There is some professional restoration, which only enhances the amazingly life-like pose, and it makes for an extremely impressive display piece, standing over 90 inches or 7½ feet high.

Estimate: $20,000-$26,000

49244   SUPERB DINOSAUR FOOT
Oviraptor philoceratops
Late Cretaceous, Campanian stage
Djadochta Formation, Central Asia

With their strange crests, weirdly recurved beaks and other features so strikingly different from other carnivorous dinosaurs, Oviraptors are among the most unusual theropod dinosaurs ever found. First discovered in 1923, recent finds show that most oviraptors were even covered with feathers and that they sat over their eggs much like modern birds, such that a time traveler going back 70 million years to the Late Cretaceous era would probably have not even realized these were dinosaurs! Their strange appearance and rapacious reputation have made the Oviraptor a staple of popular culture; it has even appeared in video games (twice improbably depicted as being able to spit poison). This exceptional foot specimen is easily one of the finest examples of its kind. Clearly suggesting the springy agile running style of the bird-like dinosaur it is, remarkably, almost 100% original, prepared to a world-class standard. It comprises the three locked metatarsals, phalanges and vicious-looking claws with well-defined blood grooves, the longest of which measures 1½ inches. The complete, articulated foot measures 9⅝ inches overall along the curve and is discretely mounted on an ebonized wooden base with a removable glass dome, 12½ inches high.

Estimate: $8,500-$10,000

49245   FINE THEROPOD DINOSAUR FOOTPRINT
Species unknown
Lower Cretaceous
Brightstone Bay, Isle of Wight, United Kingdom

The Isle of Wight off the south coast of England is home to a fine variety of fossils ranging from the early Cretaceous all the way up to the modern day (that is to say, the Pleistocene Epoch that ended a mere 12,000 years ago). The south coast of the island is lined with beautiful tall sheer cliffs of white chalk and limestone, rich in both marine fossils and rare dinosaur material, and just occasionally dinosaur tracks will be exposed along the shoreline. Worn out as three-dimensional casts from when marine sands filled the footprints the dinosaurs left in the mud, these tracks provide an insight into the life of the early Cretaceous 120 million years ago. This is an excellent specimen of a theropod dinosaur footprint, "theropoda" meaning "beast feet" and most likely belonged to a creature 8 to 10 feet tall. It is amazingly well-preserved and defined as a three-dimensional cast in shell-rich white limestone; that it had been sitting on the shoreline for quite some time is evidenced by attractively mottled colonies of modern coral bryozoans. The three toes are well defined and most likely belonged to a carnivorous dinosaur like a raptor, and the track itself measures 9 inches long by 8½ inches wide.

Estimate: $800-$1,200

49247 LARGE DINOSAUR CLAW
Struthiomimus altus
Cretaceous, Maastrichtian stage
Hell Creek Formation, South Dakota

Struthiomimus was one of the slender, fast-running ostrich-like dinosaurs that proliferated across North America just prior to the Cretaceous-Tertiary extinction event. Reaching speeds of up to 50 mph, it would have been able to avoid many encounters with the tyrannosaurids that dominated the food chain, but when cornered its large recurved claws would have been of no little assistance in warding off its attacker. This is a spectacularly large example, with an excellent woody texture and patina and deep blood grooves on either side, 5⅝ inches along the outside curve with only a small amount of restoration to the proximal end.
Estimate: $3,000-$4,000

49246   SUPERB DINOSAUR CLAW & TOE
Albertosaurus libratus
Cretaceous, Maastrichtian Stage
Horseshoe Canyon formation, Drumheller, Alberta, Canada

Drumheller is arguably one of the richest deposits of dinosaurian fossils in the world. It is home to, amongst others, the Albertosaurus, cousin to the T-rex and also a fearsome predator. This toe specimen is superb, comprising four sections, each with great bone patina and minimal restoration, terminating in the wicked curving claw. It was collected legally and comes with a disposition number; unfortunately only this toe was recovered and the rest of the beast was never found. Mounted on a metal stand, it is a great display piece with very little restoration, measuring 14 inches along the curve and standing 9¾ inches high.
Estimate: $6,000-$7,500

49248   RAPTOR HAND CLAW
Dromaeosaurus albertensis
Cretaceous
Judith River Formation, Montana

It is no surprise to learn that this small bird-like claw comes from one of the dromisauridae family of dinosaurs, the bird-like feathered raptors that flourished at the tail end of the Cretaceous period. Disagreement continues as to the exact function of the so-called "killing claw", whether it was used as a slashing weapon for disemboweling prey, that it performed more of a stabbing function, or whether perhaps it was primarily a climbing aid. Whatever its use, they are highly sought-after by fossil collectors for their evocative sickle shape, and this is a lovely example, with pale creamy gray-brown coloring and a blood groove on each side, measuring just over 1⅜ inches along the outside curve, with restoration to the tip.
Estimate: $2,200-$2,600

49249   VERY LARGE AND PRISTINE T. REX TOOTH

Tyrannosaurus rex
Late Cretaceous – 65-68 million years old
Hell Creek Formation, Garfield County, Near Jordan, Montana

Tyrannosaurus rex was the largest, most powerful carnivorous dinosaur of all time, and the largest land carnivore of any type in our Earth's history. It measured up to 43 feet in length and weighed up to 8 tons. Its massive skull measured up to 5 feet long and was lined with huge spike-like teeth that were bigger than the teeth of any other theropod dinosaur. Its skull was narrow in the front and extremely wide in the back, allowing for the eye sockets to point well forward and indicating the presence of excellent binocular vision, which would be necessary to effectively intercept its prey on the run. The neck was short and the neck muscles huge to support the gigantic skull and absorb the shock of impact during the very violent attacks that T. rex would initiate as it would slam into its prey, mouth first, at high speed. T. rex teeth were very robust so that they would more effectively transmit the energy of impact into the victim's body and gouge, rather than cut, huge chunks of flesh out of the prey as T. rex bore down with its powerful jaws. T. rex had the greatest biting force of any large theropod, so it appears that the great jaw strength was an evolutionary adaptation to its unique open-mouthed crash hunting style. The evidence clearly shows that Tyrannosaurus rex was truly the "King of Dinosaurs".

T. rex teeth have been described by a famous paleontologist as "deadly bananas" and this tooth epitomizes that description. It exhibits gorgeous, pristine surfaces and perfect serrations on both the anterior and posterior cutting edges. The tooth possesses exquisite natural luster and the most beautiful colors running from yellow-brown to reddish dark chocolate-brown, nicely accented by dark blotches and checking. Approximately 10% of the tooth surface has been restored, primarily at the base of the posterior serrate row and a ¼ section of the tooth base. This superb quality tooth measures 3¼ x 1½ x 1⅛ inches thick.

Estimate: $7,500-$8,500

49250   RARE TYRANNOSAURID TOOTH

Daspletosaurus torosus
Cretaceous, Campanian stage
Judith River Formation, Alberta, Canada

A rather rare dinosaur, the Daspletosaurus has been found in only one locality. Although unnamed, possible relatives of the same genus have been discovered further afield across North America. A tyrannosaurid theropod, it was smaller than its contemporary cousins the Albertosaurus and the T-Rex (reaching up to 30 feet in length in adulthood), but shared their characteristic anatomical features of a large heavy head, short forearms and a long heavy tail that acted as a counterweight. But the business end of the creature was its some two dozen vicious teeth, of which the present specimen is a fine example. Ovular in section it retains good enamel coverage in a warm pale gray-brown, with excellent serrations and a good root section and measures 2½ inches along the curve with no restoration.

Estimate: $800-$1,100

49252 COMPLETE RAPTOR EGG
Elongatoolithus sp
Upper Cretaceous
Central Asia

The Oviraptor, meaning "egg-seizer" in Latin, is one of the best-known examples of a mis-named dinosaur: the first specimen was discovered in proximity to a nest of these eggs and it was assumed that the raptor was a nest thief, opportunistically feeding on the unborn offspring of a Protoceratops. Further discoveries indicated that it was in fact brooding over its own eggs in an unexpected display of bird-like behavior. Nowadays their eggs are easily recognizable, with a distinctive elongated form and dimpled texture, although the vast majority on the market are crushed and partial. The present example is therefore a comparatively high-end specimen, virtually undistorted, with complete shell covering and good texture throughout (the attractive bi-colored patina is due to the different minerals in the soil in which it lay buried for 75 million years) and it is a good-sized example at 7⅝ inches long.
Estimate: $1,800-$2,400

49251 CARNIVOROUS DINOSAUR TOOTH
Carcharodontosaurus saharicus
Mid-Cretaceous, Albian Age
Kem-Kem Basin, South of Taouz, K'Sar es Souk Province, Morocco

The Carcharodontosaurus was first discovered in North Africa in the 1920's, but its remains destroyed (in Munich) during WWII. Fortunately, discoveries made in the 1990's in Morocco and Niger and a superb example of its elongated skull now resides in the Chicago Field Museum. One notable aspect of the skull is that it is chock-full of these enormous curved teeth – a fearsome carnosaur indeed. The present specimen is an excellent large example, with a wonderful woody patina of red, brown and orange, shiny enamel and excellent serrations, measuring a full 4 inches along the curve and 1⅜ x ⅝ inches at the base.
Estimate: $1,400-$1,700

49253 GIANT DINOSAUR EGG
Titanosauroidea
Upper Cretaceous
Nequén Province, Patagonia, Argentina

This enormous egg was laid over 65 millions years ago by the giant Argentinean Titanosaur. The titanosauridae were a group of sauropod dinosaurs including Saltasaurus and Argentinosaurus, successors to the giant diplodocids and brachiosaurids, sauropods who had become extinct during the lower Cretaceous period. Like their predecessors, they were giant heavy herbivores, estimated to have weighed in excess of 100 tons. The family Titanosauridae was named for the under-described genus Titanosaurus, and there has yet to be universal agreement over the details of their taxonomic definition and sub-classification due to the relative scarcity of their remains in the fossil record. If we can be sure of little else however, with such an 8⅜-inch wide egg, the mother of this unborn offspring was a dinosaur of a size quite worthy of its titanic name.
Estimate: $8,000-$10,000

49254 MASSIVE DINOSAUR VERTEBRA

Triceratops horridus
Cretaceous, Maastrichtian
Hell Creek Formation, South Dakota

Undoubtedly one of the most well-known and popular dinosaurs, the Triceratops was a herbivore that roamed in herds across North America in the final phase of the dinosaurs' existence, just prior to the Cretaceous-Tertiary extinction event 65 million years ago. This cervical vertebra is a massive specimen, indicating a creature of close to their estimated maximum size of 30 feet in length. Comprising spinal and two transverse processes (one reconstructed), neural arch and large round centrum it bears a warm woody coloring and measures 23¼ inches long, standing 21⅜ inches high on a custom metal display stand.

Estimate: $1,600-$2,000

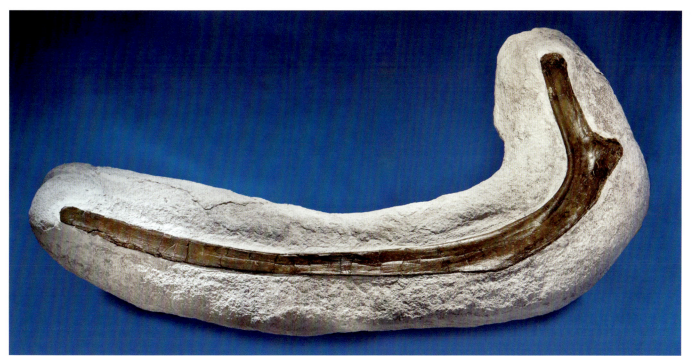

49255 LARGE TRICERATOPS RIB WITH T-REX BITE MARKS

Triceratops horridus
Cretaceous, Maastrichtian
Hell Creek Formation, South Dakota

Fossil bones tell us not only about the anatomy of the dinosaurs that lived so many millions of years ago, but often provide pathological clues as to their lifestyle, diet and even the wider context of the ecosystem in which they thrived. This is just such an example: a massive rib from the famed Triceratops, a big old Bull, complete with evidence of an attack by the fearsome and equally renowned T-Rex. The popular imagination has these two dinosaurs locked in eternal combat, the large and ferocious T-Rex feasting on the bulky herbivorous Triceratops, defending itself with its remarkable trio of skull horns. It has not been determined whether the wounds inflicted on the owner of the present specimen were fatal, but they certainly caused some serious damage, leaving well-defined grooves in the bone. With a fine dark woody patina and excellent texture, the rib is presented in a curving matrix of pleasantly contrasting pale gray, and measures an impressive 5 feet in length along the curve.

Estimate: $2,400-$2,800

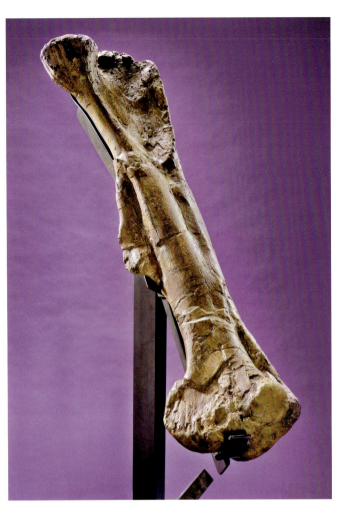

49256 HADROSAURID FEMUR

Anatotitan copie, or *Edmontasaurus annectens*
Cretaceous, Masstrichtian stage
Hell Creek Formation, Wibaux Co., mid-eastern Montana, USA

Anatotitan was the largest of the duckbilled dinosaurs, giant herbovires with a complicated taxonomic history. They roamed what is now North America during the last three years of the dinosaurs' extinction, 68-65 million years ago. This giant leg bone measures 50½ inches long and 35 inches around, with fantastic surface texture and patination, and deep warm brown mahogany coloration. It has been well restored and mounted on a solid metal display stand.
Estimate: $3,000-$3,800

49257 MASSIVE DINOSAUR DROPPINGS

Coprolite
Jurassic
Morrison Formation, Montana

One misconception regarding these rare specimens is that they were maliciously named by eminent paleontologist Othniel Charles Marsh after his arch-rival in the 19th-century American "Bone Wars", Edward Drinker Cope. In fact, in Greek, the name means "dung stone": in other words, dinosaur droppings. First described by famed paleontologist William Buckland in 1829 (from observations by the equally famed Mary Anning) these trace fossils are immensely useful indicators of dietary behavior, whether they contain the bone fragments of the carnivore's diet, or the fibers, plant material and gastroliths (stones swallowed to aid digestion) common to the herbivores; as such they also provide an excellent record of the fauna and flora of the contemporaneous ecosystem. Animal dung is highly susceptible to breaking up and dispersion, so coprolites are relatively rare in the fossil record; this is a massive example and although its source has not been identified, the size indicates it may well be from one of the massive Jurassic sauropods whose remains are found throughout the well-preserved formations of Montana. One section has been sliced and polished to show the internal structure and surprising array of soft colors, and another has been sliced to provide a stable base on which it stands 17 x 11 x 8 inches.
Estimate: $1,400-$1,800

End of Auction

Heritage Auction Galleries Staff

Steve Ivy - Co-Chairman and CEO

Steve Ivy began collecting and studying rare coins as a youth, and as a teenager began advertising coins for sale in national publications in 1963. Seven years later, at the age of 20, he opened for business in downtown Dallas, and in 1976, incorporated as an auction company. Steve managed the business as well as serving as chief buyer, buying and selling hundreds of millions of dollars of coins during the 1970s and early 1980s. In early 1983, James Halperin became a full partner, and the name of the corporation was changed to Heritage Auctions. Steve's primary responsibilities now include management of the marketing and selling efforts of the company, the formation of corporate policy for long-term growth, and corporate relations with financial institutions. He remains intimately involved in all the various categories Heritage Auctions deals in today. Steve engages in daily discourse with industry leaders on all aspects of the fine art and collectibles business, and his views on market trends and developments are respected throughout the industry. He previously served on both the Board of Directors of the Professional Numismatists Guild (past president), and The Industry Council for Tangible Assets (past Chairman). Steve's keen appreciation of history is reflected in his active participation in other organizations, including past board positions on the Texas Historical Foundation and the Dallas Historical Society (where he also served as Exhibits Chairman). Steve is an avid collector of Texas books, manuscripts, and national currency, and he owns one of the largest and finest collections in private hands. He is also a past Board Chair of Dallas Challenge, and is currently the Finance Chair of the Phoenix House of Texas.

James Halperin - Co-Chairman

Born in Boston in 1952, Jim formed a part-time rare coin business at age 15 after discovering he had a knack (along with a nearly photographic memory) for coins. Jim scored a perfect 800 on his math SATs and received early acceptance to Harvard College, but after attending three semesters took a permanent leave of absence to pursue his full-time numismatic career. In 1975, Jim supervised the protocols for the first mainframe computer system in the numismatic business, which would catapult New England Rare Coin Galleries to the top of the industry in less than four years. In 1982, Jim's business merged with that of his friend and former archrival Steve Ivy. Their partnership has become Heritage Auctions, the third-largest auction house in the world. Jim is also a well-known futurist, an active collector of EC comics and early 20th-century American art (visit www.jhalpe.com), venture capital investor, philanthropist (he endows a multimillion-dollar health education foundation), and part-time novelist. His first fiction book, *The Truth Machine*, was published in 1996, became an international science fiction bestseller, and was optioned for movie development by Warner Brothers and Lions Gate. Jim's second novel, *The First Immortal*, was published in early 1998 and immediately optioned as a Hallmark Hall of Fame television miniseries.

Greg Rohan - President

At the age of eight, Greg Rohan started collecting coins as well as buying them for resale to his schoolmates. By 1971, at the age of 10, he was already buying and selling coins from a dealer's table at trade shows in his hometown of Seattle. His business grew rapidly, and by 1985 he had offices in both Seattle and Minneapolis. He joined Heritage in 1987 as Executive Vice-President. Today, as a partner and as President of Heritage, his responsibilities include overseeing the firm's private client group and working with top collectors in every field in which Heritage is active. Greg has been involved with many of the rarest items and most important collections handled by the firm, including the purchase and/or sale of the Ed Trompeter Collection (the world's largest numismatic purchase according to the Guinness Book of World Records). During his career, Greg has handled more than $1 billion of rare coins, collectibles and art. He has provided expert testimony for the United States Attorneys in San Francisco, Dallas, and Philadelphia, and for the Federal Trade Commission (FTC). He has worked with collectors, consignors, and their advisors regarding significant collections of books, manuscripts, comics, currency, jewelry, vintage movie posters, sports and entertainment memorabilia, decorative arts, and fine art. Greg is a past Chapter Chairman for North Texas of the Young Presidents' Organization (YPO), and is an active supporter of the arts. Greg co-authored "The Collectors Estate Handbook," winner of the NLG's Robert Friedberg Award for numismatic book of the year. He previously served on the seven-person Advisory Board to the Federal Reserve Bank of Dallas, in his second appointed term.

Paul Minshull - Chief Operating Officer

As Chief Operating Officer, Paul Minshull's managerial responsibilities include integrating sales, personnel, inventory, security and MIS for Heritage. His major accomplishments include overseeing the hardware migration from mainframe to PC, the software migration of all inventory and sales systems, and implementation of a major Internet presence. Heritage's successful employee-suggestion program has generated 200 or more ideas each month since 1995, and has helped increase employee productivity, expand business, and improve employee retention. Paul oversees the company's highly-regarded IT department, and has been one of the driving force behind Heritage's Web development, now a significant portion of Heritage's future plans. As the first auction house that combined traditional floor bidding with active Internet bidding, the totally interactive systems have catapulted Heritage to the top collectible and Fine Art website (Forbes Magazine's "Best of the Web"). Paul came to Heritage in 1984. Since 1994 Paul has been the Chief Operating Officer for all Heritage companies and affiliates.

Todd Imhof - Executive Vice President

Unlike most of his contemporaries, Todd Imhof did not start collecting in his teens. Shortly after graduating college, Todd declined offers from prestigious Wall Street banks to join a former classmate at a small rare coin firm in the Seattle area. In the mid-1980s, the rare coin industry was rapidly changing, with the advent of third-party grading and growing computer technologies. As a newcomer, Todd more easily embraced these new dynamics and quickly emerged as a highly respected dealer. In 1991, he co-founded Pinnacle Rarities, a firm specialized in servicing the savviest and most preeminent collectors in numismatics. At only 25, he was accepted into the PNG, and currently serves on its Consumer Protection Committee and its Legislation/Taxation Issues Committee. In 1992, he was invited to join the Board of Directors for the Industry Council for Tangible Assets, later serving as its Chairman (2002-2005). Since joining Heritage in 2006, Todd continues to advise most of Heritage's largest and most prominent clients.

Leo Frese - Managing Director, Beverly Hills
Leo has been involved in the business of collectibles and rare coins for four decades, starting as a professional numismatist in 1971. He has been with Heritage for more than 20 years, literally working his way up the Heritage ladder before becoming Director of Consignments. Leo has been actively involved in assisting clients sell nearly $500,000,000 of material at auction, and recently relocated to Los Angeles to head up Heritage Auction Galleries Beverly Hills, the West Coast branch of Heritage Auctions. Leo was recently accepted as a member of PNG, is a life member of the ANA, and holds membership in FUN, CSNS among other organizations.

Jim Stoutjesdyk - Vice President
Jim Stoutjesdyk was named Vice President of Heritage Rare Coin Galleries in 2004. He was named ANA's Outstanding Young Numismatist of the Year in 1987. A University of Michigan graduate, he was first employed by Superior Galleries, eventually becoming their Director of Collector Sales. Since joining Heritage in 1993, Jim has served in many capacities. Jim's duties now include buying and selling, pricing all new purchases, assisting with auction estimates and reserves, and overseeing the daily operations of the rare coin department.

Norma L. Gonzalez - VP of Auction Operations
Norma Gonzalez joined the U.S. Navy in August of 1993 and received her Bachelor's Degree in Resource Management. She joined Heritage in 1998 and was promoted to Vice President in 2003. She currently manages the operations departments, including Coins, Currency, World & Ancient Coins, Sportscards & Memorabilia, Comics, Movie Posters, Pop Culture and Political Memorabilia.

Debbie Rexing - VP - Marketing
Debbie Rexing joined the Heritage team in 2001 and her marketing credentials include degrees in Business Administration and Human Resources from The Ohio State University. Debbie has worked across many categories within the company leading to her comprehensive and integrative approach to the job. She guides all aspects of Heritage's print marketing strategies – advertisements, brochures, direct mail campaigns, coordination of print buying, catalog design and production, The Heritage Magazine, and media and press relations.

Ron Brackemyre - Vice President
Ron Brackemyre began his career at Heritage Auction Galleries in 1998 as the Manager of the Shipping Department, was promoted to Consignment Operations Manager for Numismatics in 2004 and in 2009 added oversight of the entire photography operation at Heritage, wherein his department coordinates all photography, scanning and photoshopping. He is also responsible for the security of all of Heritage's coin and currency consignments, both at the Dallas world headquarters and at shows, as well as cataloging of coins for upcoming auctions, coordination of auction planning, security and transportation logistics, lot-view, auction prep and oversight for the entire shipping department.

Marti Korver - Manager - Credit/Collections
Marti Korver was recruited out of the banking profession by Jim Ruddy, and she worked with Paul Rynearson, Karl Stephens, and Judy Cahn on ancients and world coins at Bowers & Ruddy Galleries, in Hollywood, CA. She migrated into the coin auction business, and represented bidders as agent at B&R auctions for 10 years. She also worked as a research assistant for Q. David Bowers for several years.

Mark Prendergast - Director, Trusts & Estates
Mark Prendergast earned his degree in Art History from Vanderbilt University and began his career in the arts working with a national dealer in private sales of 20th Century American Art. Joining Christie's in 1998 and advancing during a 10 year tenure to the position of Vice President, he was instrumental in bringing to market many important and prominent works of art, collections and estates. Having established a Houston office for Heritage, he serves as Director of Business Development, Trusts & Estates, providing assistance to fiduciary professionals and private clients with appraisals, collection assessments and auction consignments in all areas of art and collectibles.

Jared Green - Vice President of Corporate & Institutional Client Development
Jared Green primarily works on developing institutional clients, including corporations and non-profits, and championing new ventures for Heritage's collectibles and art businesses. He maintains relationships with a number of Fortune 500 companies that have collections of rarities and fine art. Prior to joining Heritage, Mr. Green worked for several years as a business analyst with Cap Gemini-Ernst & Young in its Strategic Advisory Services group. He is a native of North Carolina and graduated with honors from Duke University with a degree in Public Policy. He completed his MBA at Emory University, where he focused on Strategy and Entrepreneurship.

Natural History Department

David Herskowitz - Director - Natural History
David Herskowitz began his career as a fine gem and mineral dealer in 1988. When he discovered a beautifully preserved insect in one of his stock of amber nuggets, he became entranced and switched his focus solely to Natural History. For many years he owned and directed a specialty business importing amber specimens before moving on to conduct Natural History auctions in New York City. An acknowledged leader in the field of fine Natural History specimens, from gems and minerals to bones and fossils, he has appeared on CNN, NBC, and ABC, and has been featured in numerous articles appearing in *The Washington Post, The New York Times, The Los Angeles Times,* and, more recently, in *Natural History Magazine.*

Peter Wiggins - Assistant Director - Natural History
Peter Wiggins is the direct assistant to David Herskowitz, Director of Natural History, where he oversees the day-to-day operations of this rapidly growing auction division. He is directly involved with every aspect of the department, including catalog production, auction operations, consignment coordination, and client service. Along with Mr. Herskowitz, Peter continues to build the department and make Heritage Auction Galleries the leader in Natural History Auctions.

Yinan Wang - Consignment Coordinator
Yinan Wang has been involved in the Natural History business for nearly a decade. His fascination with minerals and fossils began as a young man and eventually culminated into a degree in Geosciences from Princeton University. He has traveled extensively across the nation and around the world, uncovering new and exciting fossils. In his capacity at Heritage, Yinan seeks to professionally bridge the gap between commercial and academic paleontology and both acquire rare natural history specimens for auction and find examples of natural history that can be of benefit to science.

James N. Walker – Consultant – Natural History
James Walker has brings a lifetime of experience to Heritage. He has mined mineral specimens; rappelled into abandoned mines to recover them; studied extensively at museum and private collections; participated in expeditions; operated a fossil quarry, and served as an auction consultant for more than 10 years. He has been a full-time mineral dealer since 1982. His expertise encompasses a broad range, including minerals, fossils, meteorites, artifacts, gemstones and lapidary arts. He carries memberships in many mineral organizations and societies.

Mary Fong/Walker – Consultant – Natural History
Mary Fong/Walker brings her expertise in evaluating mineral specimens to her position with Heritage. She is an expert in fossil preparation and restoration and has designed jewelry emphasizing rare and exotic gemstones. She joined the world of Natural History after a corporate career, working full time in the mineral trade, side-by-side with her husband. She is a Director of the Fallbrook Gem & Mineral Society.

Cataloged by: David Herskowitz

Edited by: David Herskowtiz

Operations Support by: Peter Wiggins, Yinan Wang, Ralph Jubera, Julie Gonzalez

Catalog and Internet Imaging by: Mark Mauthner, Craig Smith

Production and Design by: Michael Puttonen, Mark Masat, Mary Hermann, Debbie Rexing

Mineral Consultants: James Walker and Mary Fong-Walker

Special Thanks: Ralph Jubera, Jorge Alvarado

Terms and Conditions of Auction

Auctioneer and Auction:

1. This Auction is presented by Heritage Auction Galleries, a d/b/a/ of Heritage Auctions, Inc., or its affiliates Heritage Numismatic Auctions, Inc., or Heritage Vintage Sports Auctions, Inc., or Currency Auctions of America, Inc., as identified with the applicable licensing information on the title page of the catalog or on the HA.com Internet site (the "Auctioneer"). The Auction is conducted under these Terms and Conditions of Auction and applicable state and local law. Announcements and corrections from the podium and those made through the Terms and Conditions of Auctions appearing on the Internet at HA.com supersede those in the printed catalog.

Buyer's Premium:

2. On bids placed through Auctioneer, a Buyer's Premium of fifteen percent (15%) will be added to the successful hammer price bid on lots in Coin, Currency, and Philatelic auctions or nineteen and one-half percent (19.5%) on lots in all other auctions. There is a minimum Buyer's Premium of $14.00 per lot. In Gallery Auctions (sealed bid auctions of mostly bulk numismatic material), the Buyer's Premium is 19.5%.

Auction Venues:

3. The following Auctions are conducted solely on the Internet: Heritage Weekly Internet Auctions (Coin, Currency, Comics, and Vintage Movie Poster); Heritage Monthly Internet Auctions (Sports, and Stamps). Signature® Auctions and Grand Format Auctions accept bids from the Internet, telephone, fax, or mail first, followed by a floor bidding session; Heritage Live and real-time telephone bidding are available to registered clients during these auctions.

Bidders:

4. Any person participating or registering for the Auction agrees to be bound by and accepts these Terms and Conditions of Auction ("Bidder(s)").
5. All Bidders must meet Auctioneer's qualifications to bid. Any Bidder who is not a client in good standing of the Auctioneer may be disqualified at Auctioneer's sole option and will not be awarded lots. Such determination may be made by Auctioneer in its sole and unlimited discretion, at any time prior to, during, or even after the close of the Auction. Auctioneer reserves the right to exclude any person from the auction.
6. If an entity places a bid, then the person executing the bid on behalf of the entity agrees to personally guarantee payment for any successful bid.

Credit:

7. Bidders who have not established credit with the Auctioneer must either furnish satisfactory credit information (including two collectibles-related business references) well in advance of the Auction or supply valid credit card information. Bids placed through our Interactive Internet program will only be accepted from pre-registered Bidders; Bidders who are not members of HA.com or affiliates should pre-register at least 48 hours before the start of the first session (exclusive of holidays or weekends) to allow adequate time to contact references. Credit may be granted at the discretion of Auctioneer. Additionally Bidders who have not previously established credit or who wish to bid in excess of their established credit history may be required to provide their social security number or the last four digits thereof to us so a credit check may be performed prior to Auctioneer's acceptance of a bid.

Bidding Options:

8. Bids in Signature® Auctions or Grand Format Auctions may be placed as set forth in the printed catalog section entitled "Choose your bidding method." For auctions held solely on the Internet, see the alternatives on HA.com. Review at HA.com/common/howtobid.php.
9. Presentment of Bids: Non-Internet bids (including but not limited to podium, fax, phone and mail bids) are treated similar to floor bids in that they must be on-increment or at a half increment (called a cut bid). Any podium, fax, phone, or mail bids that do not conform to a full or half increment will be rounded up or down to the nearest full or half increment and this revised amount will be considered your high bid.
10. Auctioneer's Execution of Certain Bids. Auctioneer cannot be responsible for your errors in bidding, so carefully check that every bid is entered correctly. When identical mail or FAX bids are submitted, preference is given to the first received. To ensure the greatest accuracy, your written bids should be entered on the standard printed bid sheet and be received at Auctioneer's place of business at least two business days before the Auction start. Auctioneer is not responsible for executing mail bids or FAX bids received on or after the day the first lot is sold, nor Internet bids submitted after the published closing time; nor is Auctioneer responsible for proper execution of bids submitted by telephone, mail, FAX, e-mail, Internet, or in person once the Auction begins. Internet bids may not be withdrawn until your written request is received and acknowledged by Auctioneer (FAX: 214-4438425); such requests must state the reason, and may constitute grounds for withdrawal of bidding privileges. Lots won by mail Bidders will not be delivered at the Auction unless prearranged.
11. Caveat as to Bid Increments. Bid increments (over the current bid level) determine the lowest amount you may bid on a particular lot. Bids greater than one increment over the current bid can be any whole dollar amount. It is possible under several circumstances for winning bids to be between increments, sometimes only $1 above the previous increment. Please see: "How can I lose by less than an increment?" on our website. Bids will be accepted in whole dollar amounts only. No "buy" or "unlimited" bids will be accepted.

The following chart governs current bidding increments.

Current Bid	Bid Increment	Current Bid	Bid Increment
<$10	$1	$20,000 - $29,999	$2,000
$10 - $29	$2	$30,000 - $49,999	$2,500
$30 - $49	$3	$50,000 - $99,999	$5,000
$50 - $99	$5	$100,000 - $199,999	$10,000
$100 - $199	$10	$200,000 - $299,999	$20,000
$200 - $299	$20	$300,000 - $499,999	$25,000
$300 - $499	$25	$500,000 - $999,999	$50,000
$500 - $999	$50	$1,000,000 - $1,999,999	$100,000
$1,000 - $1,999	$100	$2,000,000 - $2,999,999	$200,000
$2,000 - $2,999	$200	$3,000,000 - $4,999,999	$250,000
$3,000 - $4,999	$250	$5,000,000 - $9,999,999	$500,000
$5,000 - $9,999	$500	>$10,000,000	$1,000,000
$10,000 - $19,999	$1,000		

12. If Auctioneer calls for a full increment, a bidder may request Auctioneer to accept a bid at half of the increment ("Cut Bid") only once per lot. After offering a Cut Bid, bidders may continue to participate only at full increments. Off-increment bids may be accepted by the Auctioneer at Signature® Auctions and Grand Format Auctions. If the Auctioneer solicits bids other than the expected increment, these bids will not be considered Cut Bids.

Conducting the Auction:

13. Notice of the consignor's liberty to place bids on his lots in the Auction is hereby made in accordance with Article 2 of the Texas Business and Commercial Code. A "Minimum Bid" is an amount below which the lot will not sell. THE CONSIGNOR OF PROPERTY MAY PLACE WRITTEN "Minimum Bids" ON HIS LOTS IN ADVANCE OF THE AUCTION; ON SUCH LOTS, IF THE HAMMER PRICE DOES NOT MEET THE "Minimum Bid", THE CONSIGNOR MAY PAY A REDUCED COMMISSION ON THOSE LOTS. "Minimum Bids" are generally posted online several days prior to the Auction closing. For any successful bid placed by a consignor on his Property on the Auction floor, or by any means during the live session, or after the "Minimum Bid" for an Auction have been posted, we will require the consignor to pay full Buyer's Premium and Seller's Commissions on such lot.
14. The highest qualified Bidder recognized by the Auctioneer shall be the buyer. In the event of a tie bid, the earliest bid received or recognized wins. In the event of any dispute between any Bidders at an Auction, Auctioneer may at his sole discretion reoffer the lot. Auctioneer's decision and declaration of the winning Bidder shall be final and binding upon all Bidders. Bids properly offered, whether by floor Bidder or other means of bidding, may on occasion be missed or go unrecognized; in such cases, the Auctioneer may declare the recognized bid accepted as the winning bid, regardless of whether a competing bid may have been higher.
15. Auctioneer reserves the right to refuse to honor any bid or to limit the amount of any bid, in its sole discretion. A bid is considered not made in "Good Faith" when made by an insolvent or irresponsible person, a person under the age of eighteen, or is not supported by satisfactory credit, collectibles references, or otherwise. Regardless of the disclosure of his identity, any bid by a consignor or his agent on a lot consigned by him is deemed to be made in "Good Faith." Any person apparently appearing on the OFAC list is not eligible to bid.
16. Nominal Bids. The Auctioneer in its sole discretion may reject nominal bids, small opening bids, or very nominal advances. If a lot bearing estimates fails to open for 40–60% of the low estimate, the Auctioneer may pass the item or may place a protective bid on behalf of the consignor.
17. Lots bearing bidding estimates shall open at Auctioneer's discretion (approximately 50%-60% of the low estimate). In the event that no bid meets or exceeds that opening amount, the lot shall pass as unsold.
18. All items are to be purchased per lot as numerically indicated and no lots will be broken. Auctioneer reserves the right to withdraw, prior to the close, any lots from the Auction.
19. Auctioneer reserves the right to rescind the sale in the event of nonpayment, breach of a warranty, disputed ownership, auctioneer's clerical error or omission in exercising bids and reserves, or for any other reason and in Auctioneer's sole discretion. In cases of nonpayment, Auctioneer's election to void a sale does not relieve the Bidder from their obligation to pay Auctioneer its fees (seller's and buyer's premium) and any other damages or expenses pertaining to the lot.
20. Auctioneer occasionally experiences Internet and/or Server service outages, and Auctioneer periodically schedules system downtime for maintenance and other purposes, during which Bidders cannot participate or place bids. If such outages occur, we may at our discretion extend bidding for the Auction. Bidders unable to place their Bids through the Internet are directed to contact Client Services at 1-800-872-6467.
21. The Auctioneer, its affiliates, or their employees consign items to be sold in the Auction, and may bid on those lots or any other lots. Auctioneer or affiliates expressly reserve the right to modify any such bids at any time prior to the hammer based upon data made known to the Auctioneer or its affiliates. The Auctioneer may extend advances, guarantees, or loans to certain consignors.
22. The Auctioneer has the right to sell certain unsold items after the close of the Auction. Such lots shall be considered sold during the Auction and all these Terms and Conditions shall apply to such sales including but not limited to the Buyer's Premium, return rights, and disclaimers.

Payment:

23. All sales are strictly for cash in United States dollars (including U.S. currency, bank wire, cashier checks, travelers checks, eChecks, and bank money orders, all subject to reporting requirements). All are subject to clearing and funds being received In Auctioneer's account before delivery of the purchases. Auctioneer reserves the right to determine if a check constitutes "good funds" when drawn on a U.S. bank for ten days, and thirty days when drawn on an international bank. Credit Card (Visa or Master Card only) and PayPal payments may be accepted up to $10,000 from non-dealers at the sole discretion of the Auctioneer, subject to the following limitations: a) sales are only to the cardholder, b) purchases are shipped to the cardholder's registered and verified address, c) Auctioneer may pre-approve the cardholder's credit line, d) a credit card transaction may not be used in conjunction with any other financing or extended terms offered by the Auctioneer, and must transact immediately upon invoice presentation, e) rights of return are governed by these Terms and Conditions, which supersede those conditions promulgated by the card issuer, f) floor Bidders must present their card.
24. Payment is due upon closing of the Auction session, or upon presentment of an invoice. Auctioneer reserves the right to void an invoice if payment in full is not received within 7 days after the close of the Auction. In cases of nonpayment, Auctioneer's election to void a sale does not relieve the Bidder from their obligation to pay Auctioneer its fees (seller's and buyer's premium) on the lot and any other damages pertaining to the lot.
25. Lots delivered to you, or your representative in the States of Texas, California, **New York**, or other states where the Auction may be held, are subject to all applicable state and local taxes, unless appropriate permits are on file with Auctioneer. Bidder agrees to pay Auctioneer the actual amount of tax due in the event that sales tax is not properly collected due to: 1) an expired, inaccurate, inappropriate tax certificate or declaration, 2) an incorrect interpretation of the applicable statute, 3) or any other reason. The appropriate form or certificate must be on file at and verified by Auctioneer five days prior to Auction or tax must be paid; only if such form or certificate is received by Auctioneer within 4 days after the Auction can a refund of tax paid be made. Lots from different Auctions may not be aggregated for sales tax purposes.
26. In the event that a Bidder's payment is dishonored upon presentment(s), Bidder shall pay the maximum statutory processing fee set by applicable state law. If you attempt to pay via eCheck and your financial institution denies this transfer from your bank account, or the payment cannot be completed using the selected funding source, you agree to complete payment using your credit card on file.
27. If any Auction invoice submitted by Auctioneer is not paid in full when due, the unpaid balance will bear interest at the highest rate permitted by law from the date of invoice until paid. Any invoice not paid when due will bear a three percent (3%) late fee on the invoice amount or three percent (3%) of any installment that is past due. If the Auctioneer refers any invoice to an attorney for collection, the buyer agrees to pay attorney's fees, court costs, and other collection costs incurred by Auctioneer. If Auctioneer assigns collection to its in-house legal staff, such attorney's time expended on the matter shall be compensated at a rate comparable to the hourly rate of independent attorneys.
28. In the event a successful Bidder fails to pay any amounts due, Auctioneer reserves the right to sell the lot(s) securing the invoice to any underbidders in the Auction that the lot(s) appeared, or at subsequent private or public sale, or relist the lot(s) in a future auction conducted by Auctioneer. A defaulting Bidder agrees to pay for the reasonable costs of resale (including a 10% seller's commission, if consigned to an auction conducted by Auctioneer). The defaulting Bidder is liable to pay any difference between his total original invoice for the lot(s), plus any applicable interest, and the net proceeds for the lot(s) if sold at private sale or the subsequent hammer price of the lot(s) less the 10% seller's commissions, if sold at an Auctioneer's auction.

29. Auctioneer reserves the right to require payment in full in good funds before delivery of the merchandise.
30. Auctioneer shall have a lien against the merchandise purchased by the buyer to secure payment of the Auction invoice. Auctioneer is further granted a lien and the right to retain possession of any other property of the buyer then held by the Auctioneer or its affiliates to secure payment of any Auction invoice or any other amounts due the Auctioneer or affiliates from the buyer. With respect to these lien rights, Auctioneer shall have all the rights of a secured creditor under Article 9 of the Texas Uniform Commercial Code, including but not limited to the right of sale. In addition, with respect to payment of the Auction invoice(s), the buyer waives any and all rights of offset he might otherwise have against the Auctioneer and the consignor of the merchandise included on the invoice. If a Bidder owes Auctioneer or its affiliates on any account, Auctioneer and its affiliates shall have the right to offset such unpaid account by any credit balance due Bidder, and it may secure by possessory lien any unpaid amount by any of the Bidder's property in their possession.
31. Title shall not pass to the successful Bidder until all invoices are paid in full. It is the responsibility of the buyer to provide adequate insurance coverage for the items once they have been delivered to a common carrier or third-party shipper.

Delivery; Shipping; and Handling Charges:

32. Buyer is liable for shipping and handling. Please refer to Auctioneer's website www.HA.com/common/shipping.php for the latest charges or call Auctioneer. Auctioneer is unable to combine purchases from other auctions or affiliates into one package for shipping purposes. Lots won will be shipped in a commercially reasonable time after payment in good funds for the merchandise and the shipping fees is received or credit extended, except when third-party shipment occurs.
33. Successful international Bidders shall provide written shipping instructions, including specified customs declarations, to the Auctioneer for any lots to be delivered outside of the United States. NOTE: Declaration value shall be the item'(s) hammer price together with its buyer's premium and Auctioneer shall use the correct harmonized code for the lot. Domestic Buyers on lots designated for third-party shipment must designate the common carrier, accept risk of loss, and prepay shipping costs.
34. All shipping charges will be borne by the successful Bidder. Any risk of loss during shipment will be borne by the buyer following Auctioneer's delivery to the designated common carrier or third-party shipper, regardless of domestic or foreign shipment.
35. Due to the nature of some items sold, it shall be the responsibility for the successful bidder to arrange pick-up and shipping through third-parties; as to such items Auctioneer shall have no liability. Failure to pick-up or arrange shipping in a timely fashion (within ten days) shall subject Lots to storage and moving charges, including a $100 administration fee plus $10 daily storage for larger items and $5.00 daily for smaller items (storage fee per item) after 35 days. In the event the Lot is not removed within ninety days, the Lot may be offered for sale to recover any past due storage or moving fees, including a 10% Seller's Commission.
36. The laws of various countries regulate the import or export of certain plant and animal properties, including (but not limited to) items made of (or including) ivory, whalebone, turtleshell, coral, crocodile, or other wildlife. Transport of such lots may require special licenses for export, import, or both. Bidder is responsible for: 1) obtaining all information on such restricted items for both export and import; 2) obtaining all such licenses and/or permits. Delay or failure to obtain any such license or permit does not relieve the buyer of timely compliance with standard payment terms. For further information, please contact Ron Brackemyre at 800-872-6467 ext. 1312.
37. Any request for shipping verification for undelivered packages must be made within 30 days of shipment by Auctioneer.

Cataloging, Warranties and Disclaimers:

38. NO WARRANTY, WHETHER EXPRESSED OR IMPLIED, IS MADE WITH RESPECT TO ANY DESCRIPTION CONTAINED IN THIS AUCTION OR ANY SECOND OPINE. Any description of the items or second opine contained in this Auction is for the sole purpose of identifying the items for those Bidders who do not have the opportunity to view the lots prior to bidding, and no description of items has been made part of the basis of the bargain or has created any express warranty that the goods would conform to any description made by Auctioneer. Color variations can be expected in any electronic or printed imaging, and are not grounds for the return of any lot. NOTE: Auctioneer, in specified auction venues, for example, Fine Art, may have express written warranties and you are referred to those specific terms and conditions. .
39. Auctioneer is selling only such right or title to the items being sold as Auctioneer may have by virtue of consignment agreements on the date of auction and disclaims any warranty of title to the Property. Auctioneer disclaims any warranty of merchantability or fitness for any particular purposes. All images, descriptions, sales data, and archival records are the exclusive property of Auctioneer, and may be used by Auctioneer for advertising, promotion, archival records, and any other uses deemed appropriate.
40. Translations of foreign language documents may be provided as a convenience to interested parties. Auctioneer makes no representation as to the accuracy of those translations and will not be held responsible for errors in bidding arising from inaccuracies in translation.
41. Auctioneer disclaims all liability for damages, consequential or otherwise, arising out of or in connection with the sale of any Property by Auctioneer to Bidder. No third party may rely on any benefit of these Terms and Conditions and any rights, if any, established hereunder are personal to the Bidder and may not be assigned. Any statement made by the Auctioneer is an opinion and does not constitute a warranty or representation. No employee of Auctioneer may alter these Terms and Conditions, and, unless signed by a principal of Auctioneer, any such alteration is null and void.
42. Auctioneer shall not be liable for breakage of glass or damage to frames (patent or latent); such defects, in any event, shall not be a basis for any claim for return or reduction in purchase price.

Release:

43. In consideration of participation in the Auction and the placing of a bid, Bidder expressly releases Auctioneer, its officers, directors and employees, its affiliates, and its outside experts that provide second opines, from any and all claims, cause of action, chose of action, whether at law or equity or any arbitration or mediation rights existing under the rules of any professional society or affiliation based upon the assigned description, or a derivative theory, breach of warranty express or implied, representation or other matter set forth within these Terms and Conditions of Auction or otherwise. In the event of a claim, Bidder agrees that such rights and privileges conferred therein are strictly construed as specifically declared herein; e.g., authenticity, typographical error, etc. and are the exclusive remedy. Bidder, by non-compliance to these express terms of a granted remedy, shall waive any claim against Auctioneer.
44. Notice: Some Property sold by Auctioneer are inherently dangerous e.g. firearms, cannons, and small items that may be swallowed or ingested or may have latent defects all of which may cause harm to a person. Purchaser accepts all risk of loss or damage from its purchase of these items and Auctioneer disclaims any liability whether under contract or tort for damages and losses, direct or inconsequential, and expressly disclaims any warranty as to safety or usage of any lot sold.

Dispute Resolution and Arbitration Provision:

45. By placing a bid or otherwise participating in the auction, Bidder accepts these Terms and Conditions of Auction, and specifically agrees to the dispute resolution provided herein. Consumer disputes shall be resolved through court litigation which has an exclusive Dallas, Texas venue clause and jury waiver. Non-consumer dispute shall be determined in binding arbitration which arbitration replaces the right to go to court, including the right to a jury trial.
46. Auctioneer in no event shall be responsible for consequential damages, incidental damages, compensatory damages, or any other damages arising or claimed to be arising from the auction of any lot. In the event that Auctioneer cannot deliver the lot or subsequently it is established that the lot lacks title, or other transfer or condition issue is claimed, In such cases the sole remedy shall be limited to rescission of sale and refund of the amount paid by Bidder; in no case shall Auctioneer's maximum liability exceed the high bid on that lot, which bid shall be deemed for all purposes the value of the lot. After one year has elapsed, Auctioneer's maximum liability shall be limited to any commissions and fees Auctioneer earned on that lot.
47. In the event of an attribution error, Auctioneer may at its sole discretion, correct the error on the Internet, or, if discovered at a later date, to refund the buyer's purchase price without further obligation.
48. Dispute Resolution for Consumers and Non-Consumers: Any claim, dispute, or controversy in connection with, relating to and /or arising out of the Auction, participation in the Auction. Award of lots, damages of claims to lots, descriptions, condition reports, provenance, estimates, return and warranty rights, any interpretation of these Terms and Conditions, any alleged verbal modification of these Terms and Conditions and/or any purported settlement whether asserted in contract, tort, under Federal or State statute or regulation shall or any other matter: a) if presented by a consumer, be exclusively heard by, and the parties consent to, exclusive in personam jurisdiction in the State District Courts of Dallas County, Texas. THE PARTIES EXPRESSLY WAIVE ANY RIGHT TO TRIAL BY JURY. Any appeals shall be solely pursued in the appellate courts of the State of Texas; or b) for any claimant other than a consumer, the claim shall be presented in confidential binding arbitration before a single arbitrator, that the parties may agree upon, selected from the JAMS list of Texas arbitrators. The case is not to be administrated by JAMS; however, if the parties cannot agree on an arbitrator, then JAMS shall appoint the arbitrator and it shall be conducted under JAMS rules. The locale shall be Dallas Texas. The arbitrator's award may be enforced in any court of competent jurisdiction. Any party on any claim involving the purchase or sale of numismatic or related items may elect arbitration through binding PNG arbitration. Any claim must be brought within one (1) year of the alleged breach, default or misrepresentation or the claim is waived. This agreement and any claims shall be determined and construed under Texas law. The prevailing party (party that is awarded substantial and material relief on its claim or defense) may be awarded its reasonable attorneys' fees and costs.
49. No claims of any kind can be considered after the settlements have been made with the consignors. Any dispute after the settlement date is strictly between the Bidder and consignor without involvement or responsibility of the Auctioneer.
50. In consideration of their participation in or application for the Auction, a person or entity (whether the successful Bidder, a Bidder, a purchaser and/or other Auction participant or registrant) agrees that all disputes in any way relating to, arising under, connected with, or incidental to these Terms and Conditions and purchases, or default in payment thereof, shall be arbitrated pursuant to the arbitration provision. In the event that any matter including actions to compel arbitration, construe the agreement, actions in aid or arbitration or otherwise needs to be litigated, such litigation shall be exclusively in the Courts of the State of Texas, in Dallas County, Texas, and if necessary the corresponding appellate courts. For such actions, the successful Bidder, purchaser, or Auction participant also expressly submits himself to the personal jurisdiction of the State of Texas.
51. These Terms & Conditions provide specific remedies for occurrences in the auction and delivery process. Where such remedies are afforded, they shall be interpreted strictly. Bidder agrees that any claim shall utilize such remedies; Bidder making a claim in excess of those remedies provided in these Terms and Conditions agrees that in no case whatsoever shall Auctioneer's maximum liability exceed the high bid on that lot, which bid shall be deemed for all purposes the value of the lot.

Miscellaneous:

52. Agreements between Bidders and consignors to effectuate a non-sale of an item at Auction, inhibit bidding on a consigned item to enter into a private sale agreement for said item, or to utilize the Auctioneer's Auction to obtain sales for non-selling consigned items subsequent to the Auction, are strictly prohibited. If a subsequent sale of a previously consigned item occurs in violation of this provision, Auctioneer reserves the right to charge Bidder the applicable Buyer's Premium and consignor a Seller's Commission as determined for each auction venue and by the terms of the seller's agreement.
53. Acceptance of these Terms and Conditions qualifies Bidder as a client who has consented to be contacted by Heritage in the future. In conformity with "do-not-call" regulations promulgated by the Federal or State regulatory agencies, participation by the Bidder is affirmative consent to being contacted at the phone number shown in his application and this consent shall remain in effect until it is revoked in writing. Heritage may from time to time contact Bidder concerning sale, purchase, and auction opportunities available through Heritage and its affiliates and subsidiaries.
54. Rules of Construction: Auctioneer presents properties in a number of collectible fields, and as such, specific venues have promulgated supplemental Terms and Conditions. Nothing herein shall be construed to waive the general Terms and Conditions of Auction by these additional rules and shall be construed to give force and effect to the rules in their entirety.

State Notices:

Notice as to an Auction in California. Auctioneer has in compliance with Title 2.95 of the California Civil Code as amended October 11, 1993 Sec. 1812.600, posted with the California Secretary of State its bonds for it and its employees, and the auction is being conducted in compliance with Sec. 2338 of the Commercial Code and Sec. 535 of the Penal Code.

Notice as to an Auction in New York City. These Terms and Conditions are designed to conform to the applicable sections of the New York City Department of Consumer Affairs Rules and Regulations as Amended. This is a Public Auction Sale conducted by Auctioneer. The New York City licensed Auctioneer is Samuel W. Foose, No.0952360, who will conduct the Auction on behalf of Heritage Auctions, Inc. ("Auctioneer"). All lots are subject to: the consignor's right to bid thereon in accord with these Terms and Conditions of Auction, consignor's option to receive advances on their consignments, and Auctioneer, in its sole discretion, may offer limited extended financing to registered bidders, in accord with Auctioneer's internal credit standards. A registered bidder may inquire whether a lot is subject to an advance or reserve. Auctioneer has made advances to various consignors in this sale.

Notice as to an Auction in Texas. In compliance with TDLR rule 67.100(c)(1), notice is hereby provided that this auction is covered by a Recovery Fund administered by the Texas Department of Licensing and Regulation, P.O. Box 12157, Austin, Texas 78711 (512) 463-6599. Any complaints may be directed to the same address.

Notice as to an Auction in Ohio: Auction firm and Auctioneer are licensed by the Dept. of Agriculture, and either the licensee is bonded in favor of the state or an aggrieved person may initiate a claim against the auction recovery fund created in Section 4707.25 of the Revised Code as a result of the licensee's actions, whichever is applicable.

Rev. 4-15-10

Additional Terms & Conditions:
MEMORABILIA & HISTORICAL AUCTIONS

MEMORABILIA & HISTORICAL TERM A: Signature₀ and Grand Format Auctions of Autographs, Sports Collectibles, Music, Entertainment, Political, Americana, Vintage Movie Posters and Pop Culture memorabilia are not on approval. When the lot is accompanied by a Certificate of Authenticity (or its equivalent) from an third-party authentication provider, buyer has no right of return. On lots not accompanied by third-party authentication or under extremely limited circumstances not including authenticity (e.g. gross cataloging error), a purchaser who did not bid from the floor may request Auctioneer to evaluate voiding a sale; such request must be made in writing detailing the alleged gross error, and submission of the lot to Auctioneer must be pre-approved by Auctioneer. A Bidder must notify the appropriate department head (check the inside front cover of the catalog or our website for a listing of department heads) in writing of the Bidder's request within three (3) days of the non-floor bidder's receipt of the lot. Any lot that is to be evaluated for return must be received in our offices within 35 days after Auction. AFTER THAT 35 DAY PERIOD, NO LOT MAY BE RETURNED FOR ANY REASONS. Lots returned must be in the same condition as when sold and must include any Certificate of Authenticity. No lots purchased by floor bidders (including those bidders acting as agents for others) may be returned. Late remittance for purchases may be considered just cause to revoke all return privileges.

MEMORABILIA & HISTORICAL TERM B: When a memorabilia lot is accompanied by a Certificate of Authenticity (or its equivalent) from an independent third-party authentication provider, Auctioneer does not warrant authenticity of that lot. Bidder shall solely rely upon warranties of the authentication provider issuing the Certificate or opinion. For information as to such authentication providers' warranties the bidder is directed to: SCD Authentic, 4034 West National Ave., Milwaukee, WI 53215 (800) 345-3168; JO Sports, Inc., P.O. Box 607 Brookhaven, NY 11719 (631) 286-0970; PSA/DNA; 130 Brookshire Lane, Orwigsburg, Pa. 17961; Mike Gutierrez Autographs, 8150 Raintree Drive Suite A, Scottsdale, AZ. 85260; or as otherwise noted on the Certificate.

MEMORABILIA & HISTORICAL TERM C: As authenticity and provenance are not warranted, if a Bidder intends to challenge, authenticity or provenance of a lot he must notify Auctioneer in writing within thirty-five (35) days of the Auction's conclusion. Any claim as to provenance or authenticity must be first transmitted to Auctioneer by credible and definitive evidence or the opine of a qualified third party expert and there is no assurance after such presentment that Auctioneer will validate the claim. Authentication is not an exact science and contrary opinions may not be recognized by Auctioneer. Even if Auctioneer agrees with the contrary opinion of such authentication and validates the claim, Auctioneer's liability for reimbursement for any opine by Bidder's expert shall not exceed $500. Acceptance of a claim under this provision shall be limited to rescission of the sale and refund of purchase price; in no case shall Auctioneer's maximum liability exceed the high bid on that lot, which bid shall be deemed for all purposes the value of the lot. While every effort is made to determine provenance and authenticity, it is the responsibility of the Bidder to arrive at their own conclusion prior to bidding.

MEMORABILIA & HISTORICAL TERM D: In the event Auctioneer cannot deliver the lot or subsequently it is established that the lot lacks title, or other transfer or condition issue is claimed, Auctioneer's liability shall be limited to rescission of sale and refund of purchase price; in no case shall Auctioneer's maximum liability exceed the high bid on that lot, which bid shall be deemed for all purposes the value of the lot. After one year has elapsed from the close of the Auction, Auctioneer's maximum liability shall be limited to any commissions and fees Auctioneer earned on that lot.

MEMORABILIA & HISTORICAL TERM E: On the fall of Auctioneer's hammer, buyer assumes full risk and responsibility for lot, including shipment by common carrier, and must provide their own insurance coverage for shipments.

MEMORABILIA & HISTORICAL TERM F: Auctioneer complies with all Federal and State rules and regulations relating to the purchasing, registration and shipping of firearms. A purchaser is required to provide appropriate documents and the payment of associated fees, if any. Purchaser is responsible for providing a shipping address that is suitable for the receipt of a firearm.

WIRING INSTRUCTIONS:

BANK INFORMATION:
Wells Fargo Bank
420 Montgomery Street
San Francisco, CA 94104-1207

ACCOUNT NAME: Heritage Auction Galleries

ABA NUMBER: 121000248

ACCOUNT NUMBER: 4121930028

SWIFT CODE: WFBIUS6S

Your five most effective bidding techniques:

❶ Interactive Internet™ Proxy Bidding
(leave your maximum Bid at HA.com before the auction starts)

Heritage's exclusive Interactive Internet™ system is fun and easy! Before you start, you must register online at HA.com and obtain your Username and Password.

1. Login to the HA.com website, using your Username and Password.

2. Chose the specialty you're interested in at the top of the homepage (i.e. coins, currency, comics, movie posters, fine art, etc.).

3. Search or browse for the lots that interest you. Every auction has search features and a 'drop-down' menu list.

4. Select a lot by clicking on the link or the photo icon. Read the description, and view the full-color photography. Note that clicking on the image will enlarge the photo with amazing detail.

5. View the current opening bid. Below the lot description, note the historic pricing information to help you establish price levels. Clicking on a link will take you directly to our Permanent Auction Archives for more information and images.

6. If the current price is within your range, Bid! At the top of the lot page is a box containing the Current Bid and an entry box for your "Secret Maximum Bid" – the maximum amount you are willing to pay for the item before the Buyer's Premium is added. Click the button marked "Place Bid" (if you are not logged in, a login box will open first so you can enter your username (or e-mail address) and password.

7. After you are satisfied that all the information is correct, confirm your "Secret Maximum Bid" by clicking on the "Confirm Absentee Bid" button. You will receive immediate notification letting you know if you are now the top bidder, or if another bidder had previously bid higher than your amount. If you bid your maximum amount and someone has already bid higher, you will immediately know so you can concentrate on other lots.

8. Before the auction, if another bidder surpasses your "Secret Maximum Bid", you will be notified automatically by e-mail containing a link to review the lot and possibly bid higher.

9. Interactive Internet™ bidding closes at 10 P.M. Central Time the night before the session is offered in a floor event. Interactive Internet™ bidding closes two hours before live sessions where there is no floor bidding.

10. The Interactive Internet™ system generally opens the lot at the next increment above the second highest bid. As the high bidder, your "Secret Maximum Bid" will compete for you during the floor auction. Of course, it is possible in a Signature® or Grand Format live auction that you may be outbid on the floor or by a Heritage Live bidder after Internet bidding closes. Bid early, as the earliest bird wins in the event of a tie bid. For more information about bidding and bid increments, please see the section labeled "Bidding Increments" elsewhere in this catalog.

11. After the auction, you will be notified of your success. It's that easy!

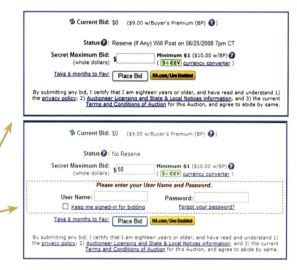

❷ HERITAGE Live!™ Bidding
(participate in the Live auction via the Internet)

1. Look on each auction's homepage to verify whether that auction is "HA.com/Live Enabled." All Signature® and Grand Format auctions use the HERITAGE Live!™ system, and many feature live audio and/or video. Determine your lots of interest and maximum bids.

2. Note on the auction's homepage the session dates and times (and especially time zones!) so you can plan your participation. You actually have two methods of using HERITAGE Live!™: a) you can leave a proxy bid through this system, much like the Interactive Internet™ (we recommend you do this before the session starts), or b) you can sit in front of your computer much as the audience is sitting in the auction room during the actual auction.

3. Login at HA.com/Live.

4. Until you become experienced (and this happens quickly!) you will want to login well before your lot comes up so you can watch the activity on other lots. It is as intuitive as participating in a live auction.

5. When your lot hits the auction block, you can continue to bid live against the floor and other live bidders by simply clicking the "Bid" button; the amount you are bidding is clearly displayed on the console.

❸ Mail Bidding
(deposit your maximum Bid with the U.S.P.S. well before the auction starts)

Mail bidding at auction is fun and easy, but by eliminating the interactivity of our online systems, some of your bids may be outbid before you lick the stamp, and you will have no idea of your overall chances until the auction is over!

1. Look through the printed catalog, and determine your lots of interest.

2. Research their market value by checking price lists and other price guidelines.

3. Fill out your bid sheet, entering your maximum bid on each lot. Bid using whole dollar amounts only. Verify your bids, because you are responsible for any errors you make! Please consult the Bidding Increments chart in the Terms & Conditions.

4. Please fill out your bid sheet completely! We also need: a) Your name and complete address for mailing invoices and lots; b) Your telephone number if any problems or changes arise; c) Your references; if you have not established credit with Heritage, you must send a 25% deposit, or list dealers with whom you have credit established; d) Total your bid sheet; add up all bids and list that total in the box; e) Sign your bid sheet, thereby agreeing to abide by the Terms & Conditions of Auction printed in the catalog.

5. Mail early, because preference is given to the first bid received in case of a tie.

6. When bidding by mail, you frequently purchase items at less than your maximum bid. Bidding generally opens at the next published increment above the second highest mail or Internet bid previously received; if additional floor, phone, or HERITAGE Live!™ bids are made, we act as your agent, bidding in increments over any additional bid until you win the lot or are outbid. For example, if you submitted a bid of $750, and the second highest bid was $375, bidding would start at $400; if no other bids were placed, you would purchase the lot for $400.

7. You can also Fax your Bid Sheet if time is short. Use our exclusive Fax Hotline: 214-443-8425.

❹ Telephone Bidding (when you are traveling, or do not have access to HERITAGE Live!™)

1. To participate in an auction by telephone, you must make preliminary arrangements with Client Services (Toll Free 866-835-3243) at least three days before the auction.

2. We strongly recommend that you place preliminary bids by mail or Internet if you intend to participate by telephone. On many occasions, this dual approach has reduced disappointments due to telephone (cell) problems, unexpected travel, late night sessions, and time zone differences. Keep a list of your preliminary bids, and we will help you avoid bidding against yourself.

❺ Attend in Person (whenever possible)

Auctions are fun, and we encourage you to attend as many as possible – although our HERITAGE Live!™ system brings all of the action right to your computer screen. Auction dates and session times are printed on the title page of each catalog, and appear on the homepage of each auction at HA.com. Join us if you can!

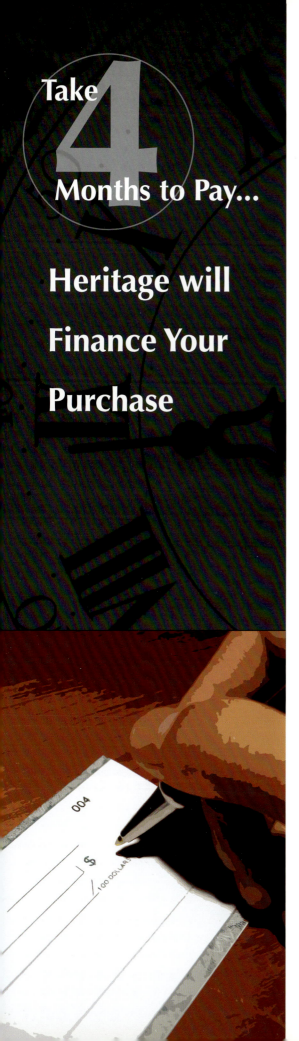

Take 4 Months to Pay...

Heritage will Finance Your Purchase

We're collectors too, and we understand that on occasion there is more to buy than there is cash. Consider Heritage's Extended Payment Plan [EPP] for your purchases totaling $2,500 or more.

Extended Payment Plan [EPP] Conditions

- Minimum invoice total is $2,500.
- Minimum Down Payment is 25% of the total invoice.
- A signed and returned EPP Agreement is required.
- The EPP is subject to a 3% *fully refundable* Set-up Fee (based on the total invoice amount) payable as part of the first monthly payment.
- The 3% Set-up Fee is refundable provided all monthly payments are made by eCheck, bank draft, personal check drawn on good funds, or cash; and if all such payments are made according to the EPP schedule.
- Monthly payments can be automatically processed with an eCheck, Visa, or MasterCard.
- You may take up to four equal monthly payments to pay the balance.
- Interest is calculated at only 1% per month on the unpaid balance.
- Your EPP must be kept current or additional interest may apply.
- There is no penalty for paying off early.
- Shipment will be made when final payment is received.
- All traditional auction and sales policies still apply.

There is no return privilege once you have confirmed your sale, and penalties can be incurred on cancelled invoices. To avoid additional fees, you must make your down payment within 14 days of the auction. All material purchased under the EPP will be physically secured by Heritage until paid in full.

To exercise the EPP option, please notify **Eric Thomas** at **214.409.1241** or email at **EricT@HA.com** upon receipt of your invoice.

We appreciate your business and wish you good luck with your bidding.

Meet the new neighbors in Beverly Hills

Leo Frese
Managing Director-Beverly Hills
Leo@HA.com
800-872-6467 ext. 1294

Shaunda Fry
Consignment Director
ShaundaF@HA.com
800-872-6467 ext. 1159

Michael Moline
Senior Vice President-
Beverly Hills
MMoline@HA.com
800-872-6467 ext. 1361

Carolyn Mani
Consignment Director
CarolynM@HA.com
800-872-6467 ext. 1677

Heritage Auction Galleries has expanded!

9478 West Olympic Blvd. First Floor | Beverly Hills, CA 90212
Monday – Friday, 9 AM – 5 PM PT | Saturday, 9 AM – 1 PM PT
310-492-8600 | 800-872-6467 | HA.com

Rare Coins ▪ Rare Currency ▪ World & Ancient Coins ▪ Estate & Fine Jewelry
Watches & Timepieces ▪ Rare Stamps ▪ Music & Entertainment Memorabilia
Vintage Movie Posters ▪ Comics & Comic Art ▪ Sports Collectibles
American & European Paintings & Sculpture ▪ Art of the American West
Decorative Arts ▪ Illustration Art ▪ Modern & Contemporary Art ▪ Fine Silver & Vertu
Texas Art ▪ 20th Century Design ▪ Photography ▪ American Indian
Americana & Political ▪ Civil War & Arms and Militaria ▪ Historical Manuscripts
Rare Books ▪ Texana ▪ Space Exploration ▪ Natural History

Receive a free copy of a catalog of your choice from any Heritage category. Register online at HA.com/CATF19375 or call 866-835-3243 and mention reference CATF19375.

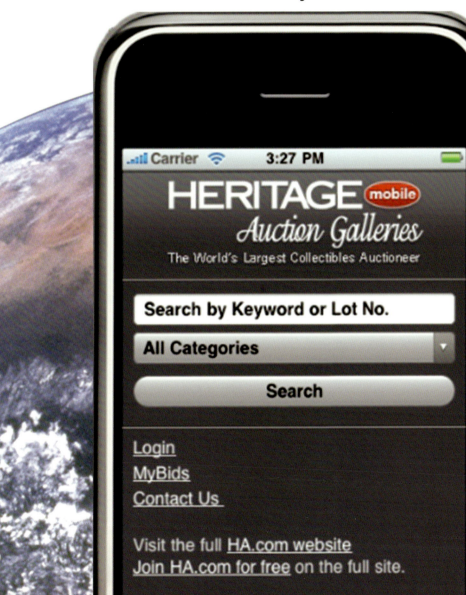
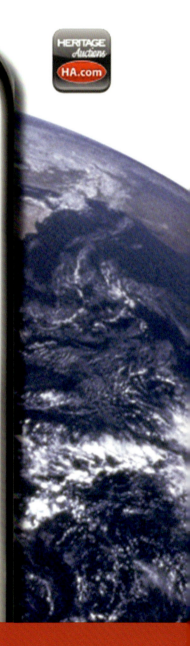

JUNE 2011
DINOSAUR AUCTION

HERITAGE

OUR MISSION

To be the world's most trusted and efficient marketplace and information resource for owners of fine art, collectibles, and other objects of enduring value

OUR VALUES

INTEGRITY
Honesty and fairness must define every facet of our business

TRANSPARENCY
We embrace clarity and freedom of information, enabling clients, partners and coworkers to make informed, confident decisions

TEAMWORK
We collaborate unselfishly, sharing credit for our accomplishments

EFFICIENCY
We seek to help clients, partners and coworkers save valuable time and resources

EXPERTISE
We never stop studying and learning, because our success depends upon providing our clients with the best possible advice

INNOVATION
We continually make our services more accessible and useful to clients, often rendering our own products obsolete by creating better ones

LONG-TERM OUTLOOK
We strive to carefully construct win-win agreements with clients and partners

HERITAGE HA.com
Auction Galleries
The World's Largest Collectibles Auctioneer
3500 Maple Avenue • Dallas, Texas 75219